3

WAY TO SUCCESS

All these are recipe every one carefully test This means that each r and remade exactly as it is given here and found delicious and practical for today's homemakers.

So read carefully the following pages and the introduction to each recipe section where aids to perfection in chocolate cookery are given. Remember that quality ingredients, properly used, are the secret.

You'll see how important it is to follow recipes exactly, to read directions all the way through, to level off each measure. The rules are just good habits. You'll find it's simple as this to have success, not just once in a while, but every wonderful time!

Could be you in this picture, serving just what folks like best—Baker's chocolate cake. You'll find some dandy family recipes in this book.

How Experts Cook with Chocolate

1. HOW TO MELT CHOCOLATE

Baker's Unsweetened Chocolate is packed in individual 1-ounce squares, each conveniently grooved into half-ounce sections to insure ease and economy of use. These squares melt quickly and easily. Cutting in small pieces is entirely unnecessary. Chocolate can be melted in several different ways. These methods are explained here. Use the one which suits your recipe and utensils.

Over hot water

The preferred method—the one that requires the least watching—is to simply place the squares of chocolate in a small bowl or custard cup over hot water. A little bowl that just fits in the top of your double boiler or teakettle is convenient for this. It is not necessary for the water below to boil. When chocolate has melted, use a rubber scraper to sweep every bit from the bowl.

Over very low heat

Chocolate can be melted in a small saucepan over direct heat. Stir constantly and keep the heat low enough to prevent scorching.

Or, on an electric range with a solid unit where the heat can be turned *very low*, chocolate can be melted right in its wrapper or on foil, directly on the unit.

If the temperature gets too high, chocolate will scorch. This is because it contains fat and starch, but little water. With too much heat the chocolate loses its aroma and develops a burnt taste.

In the oven

An economical method of melting chocolate is to make use of oven heat. Just place the wrapped squares on a pie pan or piece of foil, and set on oven rack while the oven is heating. Or use this method when the heat has been turned off and the oven is cooling. Of course, it is important not to let the oven temperature get too high or leave the chocolate in too long.

In liquid mixtures

In some recipes, especially desserts, the squares of chocolate may be combined with the liquid. Heat the mixture gradually, stirring constantly. If the liquid is milk or cream, place over hot water to prevent scorching. After chocolate is melted, beat with rotary egg beater until smooth and nicely blended.

The easiest way to melt Baker's Semi-Sweet or Sweet Chocolate is to place in a small bowl over hot water—just as for Unsweetened Chocolate. These chocolates are thick when melted and will not become thinner by melting longer.

Similarly, Dot Chocolate when called for in the recipes in this book is melted over hot water—with this difference: heat only until partly melted; then remove from hot water and stir rapidly until entirely melted.

Chocolate all through—that's Way-To-His-Heart Cake. More chocolate is rippled into the frosting from the tip of a teaspoon. See page 17.

2. COOKING TEMPERATURE IS IMPORTANT

It is important to use the correct temperature in cooking with chocolate. This is because chocolate scorches easily and the flavor is then greatly impaired. Foods containing chocolate should always be cooked over hot water or over carefully regulated heat. In baking, use the temperature specified in the recipe and *do not overbake.* Overbaking mars chocolate flavor just as much as too high temperatures.

3. COCOA AND CHOCOLATE

We do not advise substituting cocoa for chocolate—these are two *different* products. Chocolate contains much more natural cocoa butter and, for that reason, gives a richer, more flavorful dish. Then again, certain sponge mixtures, like angel food and sponge cakes, are easier to make successfully with cocoa as less of the cocoa butter is desirable.

So in this book, both chocolate and cocoa recipes are given, each carefully worked out for its product.

Should it happen, however, that you find no chocolate on the pantry shelf when you are ready to bake or prepare a chocolate dessert, you may substitute 3 level tablespoons of Baker's Cocoa for each square of chocolate. In cakes or cookies, add 1 tablespoon of shortening for each 3 tablespoons cocoa used.

4. HOW TO STORE CHOCOLATE

Keep Baker's Chocolate in a reasonably cool place. Chocolate should be kept at a temperature under 75° F. If the temperature goes above 90° F., the chocolate may lose some of its fine flavor. Exposed to excessive heat, it becomes crumbly and its appearance is marred. If the temperature is so high as to cause the paper in which the chocolate is wrapped to become oily, it is very evident that some of the cocoa butter has been lost and the chocolate has deteriorated. However, if the chocolate merely becomes gray in color during storage, its goodness has not been damaged in any way.

Old Friends Are Best

We doubt whether there's any product in American kitchens that enjoys a friendlier relationship with homemakers than Baker's Chocolate. Ask a woman about it and she'll say, "Why I've used Baker's Chocolate all my life. My mother taught me to use it when I was a little girl—and she learned about it from her mother before her. It's an old friend of the family!" You may be sure that we prize this friendliness and confidence.

It's not just an accident that Baker's Chocolate has won and held friends for over 175 years. The reason?—*consistent quality!*

Quality chocolate comes only from fine cocoa beans, properly handled throughout manufacture. A vast amount of knowledge and skill lies behind the making of a chocolate like Baker's. Choice cocoa beans are carefully selected and blended by experts. Every step of manufacture —roasting, crushing, grinding, molding, packaging—is checked and controlled to make sure that every package of Baker's you buy will be of uniformly high quality.

Don't try to skimp and save on ingredients that give flavor to your foods, for they, in particular, should be the *best*. The chances are that your chocolate dish will be only as good as the chocolate you have used in it. When chocolate predominates in your recipes, be sure it's *good* chocolate, as good as money can buy—Baker's! You'll find it wise economy in the end.

BAKER'S UNSWEETENED CHOCOLATE

Baker's Unsweetened Chocolate is a blend of fine cocoa beans, roasted, crushed, and ground between great heated rollers into a ruddy-brown liquor, satin-smooth and rich in cocoa butter. Nothing is added to the pure, fragrant liquor, nothing is removed. When this liquor is poured into molds, cooled, and finally wrapped, it makes the finished product, ready to be used by you in tempting your family's appetite.

Baker's Unsweetened Chocolate, long the favorite cooking chocolate of American homemakers, is also known as Baker's Premium No. 1 Chocolate. It is probably the oldest packaged food product in America. The well-known yellow and blue package with the familiar "Chocolate Girl" trade-mark is available in 8-ounce packages. This package contains eight individually wrapped 1-ounce squares. Each square is grooved deeply into half-ounce sections which will break apart evenly and easily. Recipes which call for "a square" of chocolate mean the unbroken full ounce, individually wrapped.

BAKER'S SEMI-SWEET CHOCOLATE CHIPS

A lively addition to the Baker line is Baker's Semi-Sweet Chocolate. Packed in chip form, this delicious chocolate has introduced a whole new field of chocolate cookery—Chocolate *Chip* Cookery!

Baker's Semi-Sweet is a smooth rich blend, with just enough added sweetening to give an interesting "half-sweet" flavor. It's a delight to cook with—provided it isn't eaten first! As a confection it appeals particularly to those who prefer a not-too-sweet chocolate. Semi-Sweet can be used in many fascinating baked desserts—desserts with bits of chocolate scattered through. These resist oven heat so that even after baking, the crunchy chips of chocolate retain their form.

Baker's Semi-Sweet Chocolate Chips are available in 6-ounce and 12-ounce packages, ready for use in cooking.

BAKER'S GERMAN'S SWEET CHOCOLATE

A long-time favorite among the quality bar chocolates is Baker's German's Sweet Chocolate. It was developed in 1852 by a man named Samuel German and is a special blend of chocolate with sugar and cocoa butter added. This is an excellent eating chocolate. You'll like it, too, for lots of special cooking uses where it's handy to have a sweetened chocolate — for making luscious icebox cakes, quick frostings, sauces, and beverages. This chocolate comes in ¼-pound bars, each carefully wrapped.

BAKER'S DOT CHOCOLATE

Another Baker chocolate unique in its field is Baker's Dot Chocolate. This superb bittersweet blend is prepared especially for home candy making. Extra rich in flavor, it has exactly the right amount of cocoa butter to give the satiny gloss and tender "break" desirable for chocolate dipping. Just enough added sugar gives it the bittersweet taste which combines so deliciously with all types of centers and makes it perfect to use as a "pour-on" over nuts, marshmallows, or Baker's Coconut. We find many people nibble this "straight," too! Dot Chocolate comes in a bar, grooved deeply into eight squares of 1-ounce each. These break off easily for use. The whole bar may be grated to melt for dipping.

NEW BAKER'S COCOA

Baker's Cocoa has always been a favorite for beverage use. Now New Baker's Cocoa is especially made for better baking too. This New Baker's Cocoa is *two-ways* better! First, it's triple-milled. This makes the cocoa lighter and fluffier, so more true cocoa flavor is released in cooking. Second, it's Dutch-processed to bring out even more full-bodied chocolate goodness.

New Baker's Cocoa is better than ever for chocolate drinks. Its ruddy brown color and rich flavor make beverages tempting . . . and satisfying.

Only the choicest of cocoa beans are selected for Baker's Cocoa. Skillful blending, roasting, and processing produce cocoa of finest flavor and quality. That is why Baker's Cocoa has been a "best seller" for years.

Most illustrious of Walter Baker's customers was Abraham Lincoln, who in 1833 had a grocery store in New Salem, Illinois. Recently, when the store was restored with all its antique interest, researchers studying Lincoln's faded records found that the only packaged advertised food product sold in the store was Baker's Cocoa.

You'll find Baker's Cocoa on your grocer's shelves today in both ½-pound and 1-pound cans.

BAKER'S INSTANT

A proud newcomer in Walter Baker's family is Baker's Instant. This is a handy sweet cocoa mix which dissolves *instantly* in cup or glass to make delicious chocolate drinks—hot or cold. It's so easy to use that the children can make their own after-school or bedtime drinks. No long stirring or hard shaking needed.

Baker's Instant patented process mixes cocoa and sugar into tiny particles that actually burst the minute liquid is added. So Baker's Instant saves time and work in making chocolate drinks.

Baker's Instant is packed in ½-pound and 1-pound cans, as well as a big 2-pound canister.

CHOCOLATE—ITS FOOD VALUE

Chocolate is a real food in itself—not just a food accessory. It is highly concentrated, small in bulk, but has remarkably high food value. Because of this, armies from the days of the Revolution through to our present-day armed forces have carried chocolate in their rations.

Chocolate is a nourishing food, containing fats, carbohydrates, proteins, minerals, and sometimes added vitamins. In addition, it is high in energy value. For this reason, many people find that some form of chocolate taken between meals helps give the "lift" they need to carry on the day's activities. A few pieces of Baker's Dot Chocolate, or German's Sweet, or Chocolate Chips nibbled right from the bag, are fine energy givers. A chocolate drink made with milk supplies extra nourishment and helps to satisfy between-meal cravings.

Chocolate has an important place in menu planning, too. Because it blends well with milk and eggs, chocolate makes possible many delicious and healthful dishes. A light meal, such as soup and sandwiches for lunch, can be rounded out nicely with a chocolate pudding for dessert. A full-course dinner can end on a happy note with a luscious chocolate cake. A "company" dinner calls for an elegant dessert such as a chocolate icebox cake or soufflé. In this book you'll find recipes to fit any menu.

Because flour packs on standing, it is important always to sift it once before measuring, then lift lightly into cup, and level off carefully.

USE QUALITY FLOUR—PERFECT LEAVENING

In this book Swans Down Cake Flour is specified for all cakes and many other baked products. In it you have a perfect cake flour. One that will give beautiful cakes with feathery, fine, even texture. The melt-in-your-mouth kind of cakes! Even the most economical cake made with Swans Down will have the fine, tender crumb of luxury cake. You can depend upon Swans Down for quality.

In all the recipes where baking powder is required, we have used Calumet Baking Powder. Calumet has a double leavening action; it contains two gas-releasing ingredients. The two leavening actions are perfectly timed and balanced, making Calumet not only unusually efficient, but also economical.

Use the exact amount of Calumet called for in the recipes—even though you may have been using more of some other baking powder. The amount the recipe calls for gives the best results in texture, grain, and lightness. If another baking powder is used, adjust the proportions as recommended by the manufacturer.

Let's Bake a Chocolate Cake

Ask people the country over what kind of cake they like best and the answer you'll get oftenest is—*chocolate!* Here is where perfection is worth striving for, because it's the kind of cake that men, women, and children love best. So let's see what the experts have to say about how to make that perfect chocolate cake!

RECIPES TO INSURE PERFECT RESULTS

An ideal chocolate cake cannot be made simply by adding chocolate to your favorite cake recipe. Because chocolate contains a certain amount of natural starch as well as cocoa butter, it cannot be added successfully to a plain cake recipe without also changing the amounts of some of the other ingredients. By using this book, you can eliminate the need for any guesswork. All of the recipes have been carefully tested in the famous Baker's Chocolate Kitchens; exact proportions have been worked out.

You'll notice in some of the recipes that slightly different amounts of liquid are suggested for different types of shortening. In these, butter, margarine, and lard give best results with a little less liquid than vegetable shortenings require. The difference is only a few tablespoons. Yet this small liquid adjustment is a practical way to keep the right balance of ingredients within the recipe.

GETTING READY TO BAKE A CAKE

When making a cake, have ingredients, pans, and oven ready before mixing. The following plan and suggestions are given for your convenience.

1. Allow shortening and eggs to stand at cool room temperature for some time before using. You will find shortening creams better and eggs whip to a greater volume when not too cold.

2. Light the oven. Be sure to note the temperature given in the recipe because correct baking temperature is very important to cake success.

3. Grease the cake pans with melted shortening. For best results, line bottom of pan with waxed or heavy paper cut to fit, then grease paper. And be sure to grease well into the corners. Use a pastry brush or piece of crumpled waxed paper for greasing.

4. Melt the squares of Baker's Chocolate in a small bowl over hot water. Do not allow any drops of water to get into chocolate for they might make it lumpy.

5. Sift flour, then place *lightly* in measuring cup and level off. *Do not pack.* Sifted flour measures more than that taken directly from the package because of the air which has been incorporated; this makes the flour light and feathery. Add salt and leavening to measured flour and sift together three times. This insures thorough blending of these ingredients by distributing the leavening and salt evenly through the flour.

Have Chocolate Sundae Cake with chocolate-on-chocolate and nuts for the frosting of two moist, light, wonderful layers. Recipe on page 32.

For chocolate cakes, pour melted chocolate over the creamy mix of butter, sugar, and egg; then blend in well with good hard beating.

MIXING CAKE—REGULAR WAY

1. Cream shortening, then add sugar in 4 to 6 additions, starting with about 2 tablespoons and increasing each addition. Cream after each amount until mixture is beautifully fluffy and light. This is *very important* in the regular method of cake making. The creamed mixture should look almost like whipped cream.

2. Add eggs—if whole and unbeaten, add one at a time, beating thoroughly. Thorough beating of the creamed mixture with the eggs is another important step in successful cake making.

3. Add the melted chocolate and blend. Remember to sweep the sides of the bowl clean with a plate scraper or flexible spatula.

4. Now add the flour and milk alternately, in small amounts, beginning and ending with flour. Beat *well* after each addition. When cakes are made experimentally, the number of strokes required at this stage is counted. The average is 300 strokes—that includes all the additions of flour and liquid. The richer the cake mixture, the more strokes required for best texture.

5. Add flavoring. Or it may be added to the creamed mixture, or to the milk—whichever way you wish.

6. If the recipe calls for beaten egg whites, beat only until they will hold up in soft, moist peaks—not until dry and crumbly looking. Then stir quickly, but thoroughly, into the batter until no visible particles remain.

7. Turn batter into the pans—the kind and sizes are specified in the recipe. Place in the oven so that oven heat has a fair chance to circulate freely around the pan.

8. Watch the time, because overbaking impairs chocolate flavor. Test the cake for doneness, using a wire cake tester or toothpick. When inserted in the center of the cake, it should come out clean and dry.

9. When cake is done, remove from oven. Place on rack to cool 10 to 15 minutes before removing from pan.

MIXING CAKE—"MIX-EASY" WAY

In addition to cakes made by the regular method just outlined, you'll find several "Mix-Easy" cakes in this book. These use a streamline method which cuts the mixing time in half. There's no creaming and only 3 minutes beating!

Yet "Mix-Easy" cakes have delicious eating quality. They are moist, tender, delicate, and *keep* fresh-tasting!

The recipes are successful for mixing by hand or electric mixer—at a low speed. These are the steps:

1. Use room-temperature shortening.

2. Sift all dry ingredients over shortening; add part of liquid. Then beat 2 *minutes.*

3. Add eggs and last of liquid. Beat *1 minute* longer.

ABOUT FROSTINGS

Most cake recipes give suggestions for suitable frostings. But if you prefer other combinations, there's full choice in the Baker's Unsweetened Chocolate frosting recipes (pages 72 to 80). A glance at the Index (last page) will show still more, made with other chocolates of the Baker line.

Scotch Chocolate Cake (1 egg)

1½ cups sifted Swans Down Cake Flour
1 teaspoon soda
¾ teaspoon salt
4 tablespoons butter or other shortening
1 cup sugar
1 egg, unbeaten
2 squares Baker's Unsweetened Chocolate, melted
* Sour milk (see below for amount)
½ teaspoon vanilla

• Sift flour once, measure, add soda and salt, and sift together three times. Cream shortening, add sugar gradually, and cream together until light and fluffy. Add egg and beat well; then add chocolate and blend. Add flour, alternately with milk, a small amount at a time, beating after each addition until smooth. Add vanilla. Turn into 8x8x2-inch pan, lined with paper and greased. Bake in moderate oven (350°F.) 40 minutes, or until done. Spread Quick Mocha Frosting (page 75) or Cocoa Frosting (page 74) over top and sides of cake.

* *With butter, margarine, or lard, use ⅞ cup sour milk. With vegetable or any other shortening, use 1 cup sour milk. To sour fresh milk, add 1 tablespoon vinegar to each cup milk and let stand in warm place a few minutes.*

Devil's Food Cake (2 eggs)

2 cups sifted Swans Down Cake Flour
1 teaspoon soda
¾ teaspoon salt
½ cup shortening
1⅓ cups sugar
2 eggs, unbeaten
2 to 3 squares Baker's Unsweetened Chocolate, melted
* Milk (see below for amount)
1 teaspoon vanilla

• Sift flour once, measure, add soda and salt, and sift together three times. Cream shortening, add sugar gradually, and cream together until light and fluffy. Add eggs, one at a time, beating well after each; then add chocolate and blend. Add flour, alternately with milk, a small amount at a time, beating after each addition until smooth. Add vanilla. Bake in two greased deep 9-inch layer pans or two greased 8x8x2-inch pans in moderate oven (350° F.) for 25 to 30 minutes, or until done. Spread Fluffy Seven Minute Frosting (page 73) or Mint Frosting (page 74) between layers and on top and sides of cake.

* *With butter, margarine, or lard, use 1 cup milk. With vegetable or other shortening, use 1 cup plus 2 tablespoons milk.*

Way-To-His-Heart Cake

• Use recipe for Devil's Food Cake (above). Bake in two greased 9-inch layer pans in moderate oven (350° F.) 25 to 30 minutes, or until done. Cool thoroughly. Spread Chocolate Seven Minute Frosting (page 73) between layers and on top and sides of cake.

Melt ½ square Baker's Unsweetened Chocolate with ½ teaspoon butter; cool. Make swirled effect on top of cake by dipping tip of teaspoon in chocolate mixture and forming half-moon swirls in the frosting.

Hail the favorite—rich, dark Devil's Food Cake, topped with swirls and whirls of Fluffy Seven Minute Frosting. Recipe is on page 16.

Chocolate Shadow Cake

• Bake Devil's Food Cake (page 16) in two 9-inch layers. Spread Seven Minute Frosting (page 73) between layers and over top and sides. Melt 2 squares Baker's Unsweetened Chocolate and 2 teaspoons butter; blend. Cool slightly; then pour from spoon over cake, letting it run down sides.

Chocolate Fudge Layer Cake

• Follow recipe for Devil's Food Cake (page 16), using 2 squares Baker's Unsweetened Chocolate. Bake in two greased 9-inch layer pans in moderate oven (350° F.) 30 minutes, or until done. Spread Fudge Frosting (page 78) or Chocolate Fluff Topping (page 92) between layers and on top of cake.

Fudge Pecan Layer Cake

• Use recipe for Devil's Food Cake (page 16). Bake in two deep 9-inch layer pans as directed. Spread Fudge Frosting (page 78) between layers and on top of cake; decorate with pecan meats. Or spread with Coffee-Chocolate Cream Frosting (page 78) and sprinkle with chopped nut meats.

Chocolate Marble Cake (3 egg whites)

1 square Baker's Unsweetened Chocolate, melted
1 tablespoon sugar
2 tablespoons hot water
¼ teaspoon soda

2 cups sifted Swans Down Cake Flour
2 teaspoons Calumet Baking Powder
¾ teaspoon salt
6 tablespoons butter or other shortening
1 cup sugar
¾ cup milk
1 teaspoon vanilla
3 egg whites

• To melted chocolate, add 1 tablespoon sugar, hot water, and soda and blend. Cool.

Sift flour once, measure, add baking powder and salt, and sift together three times. Cream shortening, add 1 cup sugar gradually, and cream together until light and fluffy. Add flour, alternately with milk, a small amount at a time, beating after each addition until smooth. Add vanilla. Beat egg whites until they will hold up in moist peaks. Stir quickly but thoroughly into cake batter.

Add chocolate mixture to ⅓ of batter. Put by tablespoons into two greased 8-inch layer pans, alternating light and dark mixtures. Then with knife cut carefully through batter once in a wide zigzag course. Bake in moderate oven (375° F.) 25 minutes, or until done. Spread Hungarian Chocolate Frosting (page 76) between layers and on top and sides of cake. Or spread cake with Chocolate Sundae Frosting (page 77).

Marble Loaf Cake

• Use recipe for Chocolate Marble Cake (above), decreasing milk to ⅔ cup. Bake in greased loaf pan, 9x5x3 inches, or square pan, 8x8x2 inches, in moderate oven (350° F.) 1 hour, or until done. Spread with Quick Chocolate Frosting or Cocoa Frosting (page 74), if desired.

Chocolate Layer Cake (1 egg)

2 cups sifted Swans Down Cake Flour
2 teaspoons Calumet Baking Powder
¾ teaspoon salt
⅓ cup butter or other shortening
1 cup sugar
1 egg, unbeaten
⅞ cup milk
1 teaspoon vanilla

• Sift flour once, measure, add baking powder and salt, and sift together three times. Cream shortening, add sugar gradually, and cream together well. Add egg and beat very thoroughly. Add flour, alternately with milk, a small amount at a time, beating after each addition until smooth. Add vanilla. Bake in two greased 8-inch layer pans in moderate oven (375° F.) 25 minutes. Spread Fudge Frosting (page 78) or Quick Chocolate Frosting (page 74) between layers and on top of cake. Or spread with Brown Velvet Frosting (page 91).

This cake may also be baked in greased pan, 8x8x2 inches, in moderate oven (350° F.) 45 minutes, or until done. Or bake in greased 9x9x2-inch pan in moderate oven (375° F.) about 25 minutes. Spread with Cocoa Frosting (page 74).

For cup cakes, turn batter into greased cup-cake pans. Bake at 375° F. about 20 minutes.

Martha Washington Devil's Food Cake

(3 eggs)

4 squares Baker's Unsweetened Chocolate
½ cup sugar
½ cup buttermilk or sour milk

2½ cups sifted Swans Down Cake Flour
1½ teaspoons Calumet Baking Powder
¾ teaspoon soda
1 teaspoon salt
½ cup butter or other shortening
1½ cups sugar
3 eggs
* Buttermilk or sour milk (see below for amount)
1 teaspoon vanilla

• Melt chocolate over hot water; add ½ cup sugar and ½ cup buttermilk and stir over the hot water until well blended. Let cool until time to use.

Sift flour once, measure, add baking powder, soda, and salt, and sift together three times. Cream shortening, add 1½ cups sugar gradually, and cream together until light and fluffy. Add eggs, one at a time, beating well after each. Add about ¼ of flour mixture, mix thoroughly; add chocolate mixture and blend. Add remaining flour, alternately with buttermilk, a small amount at a time, beating very thoroughly after each addition. Add vanilla. Bake in greased 16x10x2-inch pan, in moderate oven (350° F.) 30 minutes, or until done. When cold, trim edges, cut in half crosswise, and put together as a two-layer cake, with Martha Washington Fudge Frosting (page 76) between layers and over top and sides of cake.

* *With butter, margarine, or lard, use 1 cup plus 2 tablespoons buttermilk or sour milk. With vegetable or any other shortening, use 1¼ cups buttermilk or sour milk.*

Devil's Food Supper Cake

• Use recipe for Martha Washington Devil's Food Cake (above). Turn into greased 16x10x2-inch pan, sprinkle with coconut topping, and bake in moderate oven (350° F.) 30 minutes, or until done.

To make coconut topping, combine 3 cups Baker's Coconut, 1½ tablespoons Baker's Cocoa, and ⅓ cup sugar. Add 3 tablespoons melted butter and mix well.

Creole Fudge Cake

• Use recipe for Scotch Chocolate Cake (page 16). Bake in 8-inch square as directed. Spread Seven Minute Frosting (half-recipe, page 73) over cake. When frosting is set, pour Chocolate Coating (page 80) over cake, letting it run down sides. Keep cake in cool place until chocolate becomes firm.

Or bake in two greased 8-inch layer pans in moderate oven (375° F.) for 25 minutes, or until done. Spread sweetened whipped cream between layers and on top of cake. Sprinkle top with chocolate flakes (page 74).

Velvet Chocolate Layer Cake

• Use recipe for Chocolate Cream Dessert Cake (page 26). Bake as directed. Spread Orange Chocolate Frosting (page 75) between layers and on top of cake, or Hungarian Chocolate Frosting (page 76) between layers and over cake.

Taste the cake our *first* First Lady served at Mt. Vernon years ago—her recipe, made modern. Martha Washington Devil's Food, above.

"Peachy" Chocolate Upside Down Cake

(1 egg)

1 cup sifted Swans Down Cake Flour
½ teaspoon soda
¼ teaspoon salt
⅔ cup sugar
4 tablespoons butter or other shortening
1 egg, well beaten
6 tablespoons milk
½ teaspoon vanilla
1 square Baker's Unsweetened Chocolate, melted

3 tablespoons butter
½ cup sugar
1½ teaspoons grated orange rind
1½ cups canned sliced peaches, well drained

• Sift flour once, measure, add soda, salt, and sugar and sift together three times. Cream shortening. Add dry ingredients, egg, milk, and vanilla and stir until all flour is dampened. Add chocolate and blend; then beat vigorously 1 minute.

Melt 3 tablespoons butter in 8x8x2-inch pan over low flame; add sugar and orange rind and cook and stir until thoroughly mixed. On this arrange peach slices. Turn batter out on contents of pan. Bake in moderate oven (350° F.) 50 minutes, or until done. Loosen cake from sides of pan with knife or spatula. Turn upside down on dish with peaches on top. Serve warm, plain or with Whipped Cream Fruit Sauce (page 81), using canned peach juice.

Note: For best results, have all ingredients at room temperature before mixing.

This batter may be used for cup cakes or layer cake. Bake in greased medium cup-cake pans in moderate oven (375° F.) 18 minutes, or until done. Makes 18 cup cakes. Double recipe for two 8-inch layers. Beat batter 2 minutes.

Ice Cream Chocolate Cake

• Use recipe for "Peachy" Chocolate Upside Down Cake (above). Omit 3 tablespoons butter, ½ cup sugar, orange rind, and peaches. Mix batter as directed. Bake in greased 8-inch layer pan in moderate oven (350° F.) 30 minutes, or until done. Serve in wedges topped with ice cream and Chocolate Fudge Sauce (page 93).

Chocolate Pear Upside Down Cake

• Use recipe for "Peachy" Chocolate Upside Down Cake (above), substituting sliced canned pears for peaches.

Chocolate Pineapple Upside Down Cake

• Use recipe for "Peachy" Chocolate Upside Down Cake (above), substituting 4 slices canned pineapple, cut in wedges, for orange rind and peaches. Or use 1 cup grated pineapple.

If desired, use ½ cup brown sugar, firmly packed, instead of ½ cup white sugar in butter-sugar mixture in pan.

Arabian Upside Down Cake

• Use recipe for "Peachy" Chocolate Upside Down Cake (above), substituting 25 halves dried apricots for orange rind and peaches. Soak apricots 1 hour before using and drain; it is not necessary to cook them.

Quick Red Devil's Food Cake (2 eggs)

2 cups sifted Swans Down Cake Flour
1 teaspoon soda
¾ teaspoon salt
1¾ cups sugar
4 squares Baker's Unsweetened Chocolate
¾ cup boiling water
½ cup sour milk or buttermilk
½ cup butter or other shortening
2 eggs, unbeaten
2 teaspoons vanilla

• Sift flour once, measure, add soda, salt, and sugar, and sift together three times. Combine chocolate and water in top of double boiler; cook over rapidly boiling water until chocolate is melted, stirring constantly to blend. Remove from boiling water and add milk. Cool.

Cream shortening. Add dry ingredients, chocolate mixture, eggs, and vanilla, stirring until blended. Then beat vigorously 2 minutes. Bake in two greased 9-inch layer pans in moderate oven (350° F.) 30 minutes, or until done. Spread Mint Frosting (page 74) between layers and on top and sides of cake. Or spread with Cocoa Frosting (page 74).

Prize Chocolate Cake (3 eggs)

2 cups sifted Swans Down Cake Flour
2 teaspoons Calumet Baking Powder
¼ teaspoon soda
½ teaspoon salt
⅔ cup butter or other shortening
1⅔ cups sugar
3 eggs, well beaten
3 squares Baker's Unsweetened Chocolate, melted
*** Milk (see below for amount)**
1 teaspoon vanilla

• Sift flour once, measure, add baking powder, soda, and salt, and sift together three times. Cream shortening, add sugar gradually, and cream together until light and fluffy. Add eggs and beat well; then add chocolate and blend. Add flour, alternately with milk, a small amount at a time, beating after each addition until smooth. Add vanilla. Bake in two greased deep 9-inch layer pans in moderate oven (350° F.) 30 minutes, or until done. Spread Clever Judy Mocha Frosting (page 78) between layers and on top of cake.

** With butter, margarine, or lard, use 1 cup milk. With vegetable or any other shortening, use 1¼ cups milk.*

Swiss Chocolate Cake (2 eggs)

1¾ cups sifted Swans Down Cake Flour
2 teaspoons Calumet Baking Powder
¼ teaspoon soda
1 teaspoon salt
1½ cups sugar
½ cup butter or other shortening
*** Undiluted evaporated milk (see below for amount)**
1 teaspoon vanilla
2 eggs, unbeaten
2 squares Baker's Unsweetened Chocolate, melted

• Sift flour once; measure into sifter with baking powder, soda, salt, and sugar. Have shortening at room temperature; stir just to soften. Sift in dry ingredients. Add 1 cup milk and vanilla, and mix until all flour is dampened; then beat *2 minutes.* Add remaining milk, eggs, and melted chocolate, and beat *1 minute* longer. (Count only actual beating time. Or count beating strokes. Allow 150 strokes per minute. Scrape bowl and spoon often.)

Turn into two deep 9-inch layer pans, lined with paper and greased. Bake in moderate oven (350° F.) 30 to 35 minutes. Cool. Spread Almond Seven Minute Frosting (page 73) between layers and on top and sides of cake. Decorate top with a border of chopped toasted almonds.

* *With butter, margarine, or lard, use 1 cup plus 2 tablespoons undiluted evaporated milk. With vegetable or any other shortening, use 1¼ cups undiluted evaporated milk.*

Note: If a stronger chocolate flavor is desired, use 2½ squares Baker's Unsweetened Chocolate.

Wellesley Fudge Cake (3 eggs)

4 squares Baker's Unsweetened Chocolate
½ cup hot water
½ cup sugar

2 cups sifted Swans Down Cake Flour
1 teaspoon soda
1 teaspoon salt
½ cup butter or other shortening
1¼ cups sugar
3 eggs, unbeaten
*** Milk (see below for amount)**
1 teaspoon vanilla

• Place chocolate and water in top of double boiler. Cook and stir over hot water until the chocolate melts and thickens. Add ½ cup sugar; cook and stir 2 minutes. Cool to lukewarm.

Sift flour once, measure, add soda and salt, and sift together three times. Cream shortening, add 1¼ cups sugar gradually, and cream together until light and fluffy. Add eggs, one at a time, beating thoroughly after each. Add ½ of flour and beat until smooth. Add milk and remaining flour, alternately in two parts each, beating after each addition until smooth. Then add vanilla and chocolate mixture and blend. Bake in two greased deep 9-inch layer pans in moderate oven (350° F.) 30 minutes, or until done. Spread Fudge Frosting (page 78) between layers and on top of cake. Or spread Orange Chocolate Frosting (page 75) between layers and on top of cake.

* *With butter, margarine, or lard, use ⅔ cup milk. With vegetable or any other shortening, use ¾ cup milk.*

Chocolate Cream Dessert Cake
(1 egg and 2 egg yolks)

2 cups sifted Swans Down Cake Flour
1 teaspoon soda
¾ teaspoon salt
½ cup butter or other shortening
1 ⅓ cups sugar
1 egg and 2 egg yolks, unbeaten
3 squares Baker's Unsweetened Chocolate, melted
* Milk (see below for amount)
1 teaspoon vanilla

• Sift flour once, measure, add soda and salt, and sift together three times. Cream shortening, add sugar gradually, and cream together until light. Add egg and yolks, one at a time, beating thoroughly after each. Add chocolate and blend. Add flour, alternately with milk, a small amount at a time, beating after each addition until smooth. Add vanilla. Bake in two greased 9-inch layer pans in moderate oven (350° F.) 30 minutes, or until done. Split each layer in half to make four tiers. Spread Jell-O Butterscotch Cream Filling (page 81, double recipe) between layers and on top of cake, arranging a cut surface of cake against a baked surface to avoid slipping of layers. Chill before serving. Or spread with Coffee-Chocolate Cream Frosting (page 78, double recipe), alternating the flavors.

* *With butter, margarine, or lard, use 1 cup milk. With vegetable shortening, use 1 cup plus 2 tablespoons milk.*

Chocolate Peppermint Cake (1 egg)

2 cups sifted Swans Down Cake Flour
1 teaspoon soda
½ teaspoon salt
⅓ cup butter or other shortening
1 ¼ cups sugar
1 egg, unbeaten
3 squares Baker's Unsweetened Chocolate, melted
1 teaspoon vanilla
½ cup sour cream
1 cup sweet milk

• Sift flour once, measure, add soda and salt, and sift together three times. Cream shortening, add sugar gradually, and cream together well. Add egg and beat very thoroughly. Add chocolate and vanilla; blend. Add about ¼ of flour and beat well; then add sour cream and beat thoroughly. Add remaining flour in fourths, alternately with milk in thirds, beating after each addition until smooth. Turn quickly into two greased 9-inch layer pans and bake in moderate oven (350° F.) 25 to 30 minutes. Spread Peppermint Frosting (page 74) between layers and on top and sides of cake. Decorate with a 1-inch border of chocolate flakes.

Chocolate Nut Loaf (5 eggs)

2 ½ cups sifted Swans Down Cake Flour
1 teaspoon soda
1 teaspoon salt
1 cup shortening
2 cups sugar
5 eggs
1 cup finely cut nut meats
3 squares Baker's Unsweetened Chocolate, melted
* Sour milk or buttermilk (see below for amount)
2 teaspoons vanilla

• Sift flour once, measure, add soda and salt, and sift together three times. Cream shortening, add sugar gradually, and cream together until light and fluffy. Add eggs, one at a time, beating thoroughly after each. Add nuts and chocolate and blend. Add flour, alternately with milk, a small amount at a time, beating after each addition until smooth. Add vanilla. Bake in greased pan, 16x10x2 inches, in moderate oven (350° F.) 45 minutes, or until done. Spread Clever Judy Mocha Frosting (page 78) on top of cake, or Fluffy Seven Minute Frosting (page 73) on top and sides of cake.

* *With butter, margarine, or lard, use* 1 *cup sour milk. With vegetable or any other shortening, use* 1⅓ *cups sour milk.*

Fruited Chocolate Layer Cake

• Use recipe for Chocolate Nut Loaf (above). Bake in three greased 9-inch layer pans in moderate oven (350° F.) 25 minutes, or until done. Spread Raisin Filling (page 80) between layers and Almond Seven Minute Frosting (page 73) on top and sides of cake. For a holiday garnish, decorate with raisin clusters and toasted almonds, if desired.

Easy Red Devil's Food (2 eggs)

Preparations. Have shortening at room temperature. Line bottom of 9x9x2-inch pan with paper; grease. Start oven for moderate heat (350° F.). Sift flour once.

Measure into sifter:

1 ½ cups sifted Swans Down Cake Flour
¾ teaspoon each salt and soda
1 ¼ cups sugar

Measure into bowl:

½ cup butter or other shortening

Have ready:

⅔ cup water
2 squares Baker's Unsweetened Chocolate, melted
2 eggs, unbeaten
1 teaspoon vanilla

• Stir shortening just to soften. Sift in dry ingredients; add water. Mix until flour is dampened; then beat *2 minutes.*

Add chocolate, eggs, and vanilla and beat *1 minute* longer. (Count only actual beating time or strokes. Allow about 150 full strokes per minute. Scrape bowl often.)

Baking. Turn batter into pan. Bake in moderate oven (350° F.) 45 minutes. Top with Cream Cheese Frosting (page 77).

Golden Cream Chocolate Cake (2 eggs)

2 cups sifted Swans Down Cake Flour
1 ¼ teaspoons soda
¾ teaspoon salt
½ cup butter or other shortening
1 ½ cups firmly packed brown sugar
2 eggs, unbeaten
3 squares Baker's Unsweetened Chocolate, melted
*** Sour milk or buttermilk (see below for amount)**
1 teaspoon vanilla

• Sift flour once, measure into sifter with soda and salt, and sift together three times. Cream shortening, add sugar gradually, and cream together until light and fluffy. Add eggs, one at a time, beating thoroughly after each. Then add chocolate and blend. Add flour, alternately with milk, a small amount at a time, beating after each addition until smooth. Add vanilla.

Bake in two deep 9-inch layer pans, lined with paper and greased, in moderate oven (350° F.) 30 minutes, or until done. Spread Golden Cream Filling (page 80) between layers and Quick Chocolate Frosting (page 74) over cake.

* *With butter, margarine, or lard, use 1 cup sour milk. With vegetable shortening, use 1 cup plus 2 tablespoons sour milk. To sour fresh milk, add 1 tablespoon vinegar to each cup milk; let stand in warm place for a few minutes.*

Chocolate Apricot Dessert Cake

• Use recipe for Golden Cream Chocolate Cake (above), decreasing milk to ¾ cup. Add ¾ cup cooked dried apricots, drained and coarsely cut, to batter. Bake as directed. Spread sweetened whipped cream between layers and on top of cake. To decorate, dip ends of apricot halves in melted chocolate and arrange on top of cake.

Dribbles of melted chocolate on a fluffy white frosting form intriguing patterns on Chocolate Shadow Cake. Recipe on page 18.

Cocoa Devil's Food Cake (3 eggs)

2 cups sifted Swans Down Cake Flour
1 teaspoon Calumet Baking Powder
¾ teaspoon salt
1 teaspoon soda
½ cup Baker's Cocoa
1½ cups sugar
½ cup butter or other shortening
½ cup water
1 teaspoon vanilla
¾ cup sour milk or buttermilk*
3 eggs, unbeaten

• Sift flour once; measure into sifter with baking powder, salt, soda, cocoa, and sugar. Have shortening at room temperature; stir just to soften. Sift in dry ingredients. Add water, vanilla, and ¼ cup of the sour milk. Mix until all flour is dampened; then beat *2 minutes*. Add remaining milk and eggs; beat *1 minute* longer.

Turn into two deep 9-inch layer pans, lined with paper and greased. Bake in moderate oven (350° F.) 30 to 35 minutes. Cool. Spread with Cream Cheese Frosting (page 77).

* *To sour fresh milk, place 1½ tablespoons vinegar in a measuring cup and add milk to make ¾ cup. Let stand in warm place for a few minutes.*

Deep Dark Chocolate Cake (2 egg yolks)

2 cups sifted Swans Down Cake Flour
¾ teaspoon salt
4 squares Baker's Unsweetened Chocolate
4 tablespoons butter or other shortening
2 cups sugar
2 egg yolks, unbeaten
1¾ cups milk . . . at room temperature
1 teaspoon vanilla
1 teaspoon soda

• Sift flour once, measure into sifter, add salt. Set aside.

Melt chocolate and shortening over hot water. Turn into mixing bowl or electric mixer bowl. *Cool* to room temperature. (This is important.) Then add sugar and mix well. Mix together egg yolks and 1 cup of the milk; add to chocolate mixture and blend. Sift in flour, mix until all flour is dampened, then beat *1 minute* at low speed of electric mixer or about 150 strokes by hand. Add vanilla and ½ cup more of the milk; stir until smooth. Dissolve soda in remaining ¼ cup milk. Stir into batter quickly and thoroughly. (Batter is thin.)

Turn into two greased 9-inch layer pans. Bake in moderate oven (350° F.) 30 minutes, or until done. Spread Raisin Nut Filling (page 80, half recipe) between layers and Seven Minute Frosting (half recipe, page 73) over cake. Or bake in 13x9x2-inch pan ¾ hour. Top with Quick Mocha Frosting (page 75).

Note: Cake may be mixed entirely in a 2-quart double boiler. Melt chocolate and shortening first; cool. Then proceed.

Delicious Chocolate Cottage Pudding

3 squares Baker's Unsweetened Chocolate, melted
4 tablespoons sugar
3 tablespoons hot water
¼ teaspoon soda

2 cups sifted Swans Down Cake Flour
2 teaspoons Calumet Baking Powder
½ teaspoon salt
¾ cup sugar
5 tablespoons butter or other shortening
1 egg, unbeaten
¾ cup milk
½ teaspoon vanilla

• To melted chocolate, add 4 tablespoons sugar, water, and soda and blend. Cool.

Sift flour once, measure, add baking powder, salt, and ¾ cup sugar, and sift together three times. Cream shortening. Add dry ingredients, egg, milk, chocolate mixture, and vanilla; stir until all flour is dampened. Then beat vigorously 1 minute. Bake in greased 9-inch tube pan in slow oven (325° F.) 55 minutes, or until done. Serve warm or cold with Chocolate Walnut Cream or Fluffy Chocolate Sauce (page 83).

This pudding may be baked in greased pan, 8x8x2 inches, in slow oven (325° F.) 50 minutes, or until done. Or bake in greased large cup-cake pans in moderate oven (350° F.) 20 minutes, or until done. Serve with Chocolate Mint Sauce (page 83) or any other favorite pudding sauce. Makes 15 cup cakes.

Note: Have ingredients at room temperature before mixing.

Chocolate Cherry Cake (1 egg)

1½ cups sifted Swans Down Cake Flour
1 teaspoon soda
¼ teaspoon salt
1 cup sugar
⅓ cup butter or other shortening
⅔ cup buttermilk or sour milk*
1 egg, unbeaten
2 tablespoons maraschino cherry juice
¼ cup finely chopped maraschino cherries
1 square Baker's Unsweetened Chocolate, melted

• Sift flour once; measure into sifter with soda, salt, and sugar. Have shortening at room temperature; stir just to soften. Sift in dry ingredients. Add milk and mix until all flour is dampened; then beat *2 minutes*. Add egg, cherry juice, cherries, and melted chocolate, and beat *1 minute* longer. (Count only actual beating time. Or count beating strokes. Allow 150 strokes per minute. Scrape bowl and spoon often.)

Turn into two deep 8-inch layer pans, lined on bottoms with paper. Bake in a moderate oven (350° F.) 25 minutes, or until done. Cool. Spread Cherry Four Minute Frosting (page 77) between layers and over top and sides of cake.

**To sour fresh milk, place 4 teaspoons vinegar in cup; add milk to ⅔ mark. Let stand in warm place for a few minutes.*

Chocolate Sundae Cake (3 egg whites)

2½ cups sifted Swans Down Cake Flour
3 teaspoons Calumet Baking Powder
1 teaspoon salt
1½ cups sugar
½ cup shortening
1 cup milk
1½ teaspoons vanilla
¼ teaspoon almond extract
3 egg whites, unbeaten

• Sift flour once; measure into sifter with baking powder, salt, and sugar. Have the shortening at room temperature; stir just to soften. Sift in dry ingredients. Add ¾ cup of the milk and the flavorings and mix until all flour is dampened. Then *beat 2 minutes* at a low speed of electric mixer, or 300 vigorous strokes by hand. Add egg whites and remaining milk;

beat 1 minute longer in mixer or 150 strokes by hand. (Count only actual beating time or strokes. Scrape bowl and beater or spoon often.) Pour the batter into two deep 9-inch layer pans, which have been lined on the bottoms with paper. Bake in moderate oven (350° F.) 20 to 25 minutes. When cool, spread with Chocolate Sundae Frosting (page 77).

Mocha Chocolate Tier Cake

• Use recipe for Chocolate Sundae Cake (above). Bake as directed. Cool. Split layers horizontally and put together as four-layer cake. Between two top and two bottom layers spread Chocolate Cream Filling (page 81), adding ¼ cup walnut meats to filling. Between middle layers and over top of cake spread Clever Judy Mocha Frosting (page 78).

Note: Make Clever Judy Mocha Frosting with 2 egg yolks instead of 1 whole egg, to use some of yolks left from cake.

Too luscious to miss! This fresh, rich, chocolate sponge is filled with almond custard then chocolate coated. See Chocolate Roll, page 35.

Honey Chocolate Cake (2 eggs)

2 cups sifted Swans Down Cake Flour
1½ teaspoons soda
½ teaspoon salt
½ cup butter or other shortening
1¼ cups honey
2 eggs, unbeaten
3 squares Baker's Unsweetened Chocolate, melted
* Water (see below for amount)
1 teaspoon vanilla

• Sift flour once, measure, add soda and salt, and sift together three times. Cream shortening, add honey very gradually, by tablespoons at first, beating very hard after each addition to keep mixture thick. Add ¼ of flour and beat until smooth. Add eggs, one at a time, beating well after each. Add chocolate; blend. Add remaining flour in thirds, alternately with water, beating very well after each addition. Add vanilla. Bake in two greased 9-inch layer pans in moderate oven (350° F.) about 35 minutes. Spread with Cream Cheese Frosting (page 77) or Seven Minute Frosting (page 73).

* *With butter, margarine, or lard, use ⅔ cup water. With vegetable or any other shortening, use ¾ cup water.*

San Antonio Cocoa Cake (2 eggs)

½ cup Baker's Cocoa
½ cup sugar
½ cup sour milk or buttermilk
2¼ cups sifted Swans Down Cake Flour
1 teaspoon soda
1 teaspoon salt
½ cup butter or other shortening
1¼ cups sugar
2 eggs, unbeaten
* Sour milk or buttermilk (see below for amount)
1 teaspoon vanilla

• Combine ½ cup cocoa and ½ cup sugar in small bowl. Add ½ cup sour milk or buttermilk; blend until smooth. Set aside.

Sift flour once, measure, add soda and salt. Sift together three times. Cream shortening, add 1¼ cups sugar gradually; cream together until light and fluffy. Add eggs, one at a time, beating well after each. Add flour, alternately with milk, a small amount at a time, beating after each addition until smooth. Add vanilla. Add cocoa mixture and blend. Turn into two deep 9-inch layer pans, lined on bottoms with paper and greased. Bake in moderate oven (350° F.) 35 minutes. Cool. Spread with Cocoa Whipped Cream (page 110, double recipe).

* *With butter, margarine, or lard, use 7/8 cup sour milk. With vegetable or any other shortening, use 1 cup sour milk.*

Chocolate Roll (5 eggs)

3/4 cup sifted Swans Down Cake Flour
1/2 teaspoon Calumet Baking Powder
1/2 teaspoon salt
3/4 cup sugar
5 eggs, beaten until thick and light

2 squares Baker's Unsweetened Chocolate
1/4 cup cold water
1/4 teaspoon soda
2 tablespoons sugar

• Measure sifted flour, add baking powder and salt, and sift again. Add 3/4 cup sugar to well beaten eggs, a tablespoon at a time, beating after each until blended. Add flour mixture all at once and blend in with spatula.

Melt chocolate over hot water. Remove from hot water and immediately add cold water, soda, and 2 tablespoons of sugar. Blend. Quickly stir into batter, blending well.

Pour into 15½x10½x1-inch pan which has been greased, lined on bottom with paper, and greased again. Bake in a moderate oven (350° F.) 18 to 20 minutes. Turn out immediately on clean towel, sprinkled with confectioners' sugar. Remove paper. Cut off crisp edges. Roll cake, rolling towel up in the cake. Let cool on cake rack for 30 minutes. Then unroll carefully. Spread with Golden Cream Filling (page 80) and roll again. Top with Chocolate Coating (page 80).

Butterscotch Chocolate Tier Cake

• Use recipe for Chocolate Roll (above). Bake cake as directed. Cool. Cut in half lengthwise, then crosswise. Put together as four-layer cake, matching edges and placing plain layer on top. Spread Jell-O Butterscotch Cream Filling (page 81) between layers. Chill thoroughly before serving.

Chocolate Pound Cake (3 eggs and 1 egg yolk)

2¾ cups sifted Swans Down Cake Flour
¾ teaspoon cream of tartar
½ teaspoon soda
1½ teaspoons salt
1¾ cups sugar
1 cup butter or other shortening (at room temperature)
* Milk (see below for amount)
1 teaspoon vanilla
3 eggs and 1 egg yolk, unbeaten
3 squares Baker's Unsweetened Chocolate, melted

• Sift flour once; measure into sifter with other dry ingredients. Stir shortening just to soften. Sift in dry ingredients. Add milk and vanilla; mix until all flour is dampened. Then *beat 2 minutes.* Add eggs and chocolate and *beat 1 minute* longer. (Count only actual beating time or strokes. Allow 150 strokes per minute. Scrape bowl and spoon often.)

Pour into 9-inch tube pan, lined on bottom with paper. Bake in moderate oven (350° F.) 60 to 70 minutes.

* *With butter, margarine, or lard, use ⅔ cup milk. With vegetable shortening, use 1 cup minus 2 tablespoons milk.*

Marble Angel Food Cake (8 to 10 egg whites)

1 cup sifted Swans Down Cake Flour
2 tablespoons Baker's Cocoa
1¼ cups sifted sugar
1 cup egg whites
¼ teaspoon salt
1 teaspoon cream of tartar
1 teaspoon vanilla and ¼ teaspoon almond extract

• Sift flour once; measure. To ½ cup flour, add cocoa and ¼ cup sugar and sift together four times. Sift remaining ½ cup flour four times. Beat egg whites and salt with rotary egg beater or flat wire whisk. When foamy, add cream of tartar and continue beating until stiff enough to hold up in peaks, but not dry. Add remaining 1 cup sugar, 2 tablespoons at a time, beating with rotary egg beater or whisk after each addition until sugar is *just* blended. Fold in flavoring.

Divide mixture in two parts. To one, fold in flour. To other, fold in flour and cocoa mixture. Put by tablespoons into ungreased 9-inch angel food pan, alternating white and dark mixtures. Bake in slow oven (325° F.) 45 to 50 minutes. Remove from oven and invert pan 1 hour, or until cold. If desired, spread with Clever Judy Mocha Frosting (page 78) or with Hungarian Chocolate Frosting (page 76).

All-Chocolate Cake

• Use recipe for Easy Red Devil's Food (page 28). Turn into two greased round 8-inch layer pans. Bake in moderate oven (350° F.) 25 to 30 minutes. Spread Hungarian Chocolate Frosting (page 76) between layers and over top and sides of cake. If desired, decorate with walnuts or pecans.

New Year's Clock Cake. Frost cake smoothly. With decorating frosting in cake decorator print clock numerals around top of cake, then make clock hands pointing to almost midnight. (For decorating frosting, beat 1 egg white, gradually adding 1 to 1½ cups sifted confectioners' sugar.)

This laughing Jack-O is sitting right on top of the party. A happy finish for Chocolate Tarts and for a jolly Hallowe'en. Recipe, page 48.

Little Cakes are Always Welcome

One of the delightful features of small chocolate cakes and cookies is their versatility. The young people away love to receive them from the home folks. They're indispensable for picnics, and great stand-bys for after-school snacks and for whipped-up-in-a-hurry suppers. They're equally at home at elaborate teas and in the good old-fashioned cooky jar.

In some households, lunches for school or shop are packed every day. Small cakes and cookies fit neatly and appetizingly into lunch boxes. And don't forget how men and children feel about *chocolate*!

So we've given you a wide variety of our favorites. Many are quite inexpensive and easy to mix—desirable traits in foods that are baked by the dozens and seem to vanish almost before they reach the table!

Chocolate Squares or Cookies

1½ cups sifted flour
1½ teaspoons Calumet Baking Powder
½ teaspoon salt
3 squares Baker's Unsweetened Chocolate
4 tablespoons butter or other shortening
1 cup sugar
1 egg, unbeaten
¾ cup milk
½ teaspoon vanilla

• Sift flour once, measure, add baking powder and salt, and sift together three times. Melt chocolate and shortening over hot water; cool to lukewarm. Add sugar and mix well. Add egg and beat thoroughly. Add flour, alternately with milk, stirring only to blend. Add vanilla.

For squares, spread in two greased 9x9x2-inch pans and bake in moderate oven (375° F.) 12 minutes, or until done. Let cool in pan; when almost cool, cut in squares. Remove from pan. Makes 50 squares.

For cookies, drop from teaspoon on ungreased baking sheet. Bake in moderate oven (375° F.) 9 minutes, or until done. Cool slightly; remove from pan. Makes 3 dozen cookies.

Chocolate Nut Squares or Cookies

• Use recipe for Chocolate Squares or Cookies (above). Add 1 cup chopped walnut meats to batter. Bake as directed. Cool. Spread with Quick Chocolate Frosting (page 74), if desired.

Chocolate Fruit Squares or Cookies

• Use recipe for Chocolate Squares or Cookies (above). Add ⅔ cup chopped dates or chopped raisins and ⅔ cup chopped nut meats to batter. Bake as directed.

Black and White Cup Cakes

3 tablespoons sugar
3 tablespoons water
1½ squares Baker's Unsweetened Chocolate
¼ teaspoon soda

2 cups sifted Swans Down Cake Flour
2 teaspoons Calumet Baking Powder
½ teaspoon salt
⅓ cup butter or other shortening
¾ cup sugar
2 egg whites, unbeaten
⅔ cup milk
1 teaspoon vanilla

• Combine sugar, water, and chocolate in saucepan and cook over low flame until thick and smooth, stirring constantly. Stir in soda; cool slightly.

Sift flour once, measure, add baking powder and salt, and sift together three times. Cream shortening, add sugar gradually, and cream together until light and fluffy. Add egg whites, one at a time, beating very thoroughly after each. Add flour, alternately with milk, a small amount at a time, beating after each addition until smooth. Add vanilla. Divide batter in two parts; to one part, add chocolate mixture, stirring until blended. Put by teaspoons into greased cup-cake pans, alternating light and dark mixtures. Bake in moderate oven (375° F.) 20 minutes, or until done. Spread tops with Hungarian Chocolate Frosting (page 76, ½ recipe). Makes 16 large cup cakes.

Or spread with Almond Seven Minute Frosting (½ recipe, page 73). When set, cover with Chocolate Coating (page 80).

Brownies

⅔ cup sifted flour
½ teaspoon Calumet Baking Powder
¼ teaspoon salt
⅓ cup butter or other shortening
2 squares Baker's Unsweetened Chocolate
1 cup sugar
2 eggs, well beaten
½ cup chopped walnuts or pecans
1 teaspoon vanilla

• Sift flour once, measure, add baking powder and salt, and sift again. Melt the shortening and chocolate over hot water. Add sugar gradually to eggs, beating thoroughly, then add chocolate mixture and blend. Add flour and mix well, then add nuts and vanilla. Decorate with whole nuts, if desired. Bake in greased pan, 8x8x2 inches, in moderate oven (350° F.) 25 minutes. Cool in pan; then cut in squares or rectangles. Makes about 20 brownies.

For Indians, use 3 eggs in above recipe and add ½ cup cut dates. Spread in two greased 8x8-inch pans. Bake as directed.

Toasted Coconut Brownies

• Use recipe for Brownies (above), omitting the nuts. Add ¾ cup Baker's Coconut, finely chopped, to batter. Cover with topping made by mixing thoroughly ¾ cup coconut with 1 tablespoon sugar and 2 teaspoons melted butter. Bake and cut as directed for Brownies.

Chocolate Cookies

2 cups sifted flour
1½ teaspoons Calumet Baking Powder
½ teaspoon soda
¼ teaspoon salt
½ teaspoon cinnamon
½ cup butter or other shortening
1 cup sugar
2 eggs, well beaten
3 squares Baker's Unsweetened Chocolate, melted

• Sift flour once, measure, add baking powder, soda, salt, and cinnamon, and sift three times. Cream shortening, add sugar gradually, creaming until light and fluffy. Add eggs and chocolate; beat well. Add flour, a small amount at a time, mixing well after each addition. Chill thoroughly. Roll ⅛ inch thick on lightly floured board and cut with floured cooky cutter; sprinkle with sugar or decorate for holidays. Bake on ungreased baking sheet in moderate oven (350° F.) 9 minutes. Makes 6 dozen 2½-inch cookies.

For holidays, cut cookies in fancy shapes. Decorate, using granulated sugar, mixture of sugar and cinnamon, red or green sugar; halved or finely chopped almonds (blanched), pecans, walnuts, or cashews; tiny colored candies, small red wintergreen or cinnamon candies, candied caraway seeds, or silver dragées; or raisins, currants, strips of dates, dried apricots, citron, or candied pineapple; or candied orange, grapefruit, or lemon peel. Cut strips with sharp scissors.

The illustration below suggests attractive shapes and decorating ideas to use for holiday cookies.

It's fun, takes only a bit longer, yet means so much more to have holiday cookies really look the part. See Chocolate Cookies, above.

Chocolate Icebox Cookies

3½ cups sifted flour
3½ teaspoons Calumet Baking Powder
1½ teaspoons salt
1 cup soft butter or other shortening
1½ cups sugar
2 eggs, unbeaten
4 squares Baker's Unsweetened Chocolate, melted
1 teaspoon vanilla
1½ cups broken walnut meats

• Sift flour once, measure, add baking powder and salt, and sift again. Combine shortening, sugar, eggs, chocolate, and vanilla, beating with spoon until blended; add nuts. Add flour gradually, mixing well after each addition. Divide dough in two parts; shape in rolls, 2 inches in diameter, rolling each in waxed paper. Chill overnight, or until firm enough to slice. Cut in ⅛-inch slices; bake on ungreased baking sheet in moderate oven (350° F.) 10 minutes, or until done. Makes about 13 dozen icebox cookies.

Chocolate Pinwheels

2 cups sifted flour
1 teaspoon Calumet Baking Powder
½ teaspoon salt
½ cup butter or other shortening
⅔ cup sugar
1 egg, unbeaten
1 tablespoon milk
1 square Baker's Unsweetened Chocolate, melted

• Sift flour once, measure, add baking powder and salt, and sift again. Cream shortening, add sugar gradually, and cream together until light and fluffy. Add egg and milk; beat well. Add flour, in small amounts, mixing well after each addition. Divide dough in two parts. To one part, add chocolate and blend. Chill until firm enough to roll.

Roll each half on floured waxed paper into rectangular sheet, ⅛ inch thick. Chill. Place plain sheet over chocolate sheet; then roll as for jelly roll. Chill overnight, or until firm enough to slice. Cut in ⅛-inch slices. Bake on ungreased baking sheet in moderate oven (375° F.) 10 minutes, or until done. Makes 5 dozen pinwheels.

Chocolate Crispies

1 square Baker's Unsweetened Chocolate
¼ cup butter or other shortening
½ cup sugar
1 egg, unbeaten
¼ cup sifted flour
⅛ teaspoon salt
¼ teaspoon vanilla
¼ cup nut meats, finely chopped

• Melt chocolate and shortening over hot water. Remove from heat; add sugar, egg, flour, salt, and vanilla, and beat well. Spread mixture in thin layer in two greased pans, 8x8x2 inches. Sprinkle with nuts. Bake in hot oven (400° F.) 12 to 15 minutes. While warm, mark in 2-inch squares. Cool and break in squares. Makes 2 dozen crispies.

Butterscotch Surprise Cakes

1½ cups sifted Swans Down Cake Flour
1½ teaspoons Calumet Baking Powder
½ teaspoon salt
⅓ cup butter or other shortening
1 cup sugar
2 eggs, well beaten
2 squares Baker's Unsweetened Chocolate, melted
½ cup milk
1 teaspoon vanilla

• Sift flour once, measure, add baking powder and salt, and sift together three times. Cream shortening, add sugar gradually, and cream together until light and fluffy. Add eggs and beat well; then add chocolate and blend. Add flour, alternately with milk, a small amount at a time, beating after each addition until smooth. Add vanilla. Turn into greased large cup-cake pans, filling them about ⅔ full. Bake in moderate oven (350° F.) 20 to 25 minutes, or until done. Makes 1 dozen.

When cakes are cool, remove cone-shaped piece from center of each cup cake. Fill hollow with Jell-O Butterscotch Cream Filling (page 81) and replace top.

Other fluffy fillings or soft frostings may be used to fill Surprise Cakes; or these chocolate cup cakes may be served plain, frosted, or topped with a sauce.

Chocolate Chew Ice Cream Sandwich

½ cup sifted flour
½ teaspoon Calumet Baking Powder
¼ teaspoon salt
4 tablespoons butter or other shortening
1 cup sugar
2 egg yolks, well beaten
2 squares Baker's Unsweetened Chocolate, melted
1 teaspoon vanilla
2 egg whites

• Sift flour once, measure, add baking powder and salt, and sift together three times. Cream shortening, add sugar gradually, and cream together well. Add egg yolks and mix well. Add chocolate and vanilla, and blend. Add flour and mix well. Beat egg whites until stiff enough to hold up in moist peaks, but not dry. Fold into chocolate mixture. Turn into greased 9x9-inch pan. Bake in slow oven (325° F.) 30 to 35 minutes. Cool. Cut in 2¼-inch squares.

To serve, place vanilla ice cream between two squares and pour Chocolate Fudge Sauce (page 93) or Chocolate Mint Sauce (page 83) over top. Or use other flavors of ice cream, such as butter-pecan, coffee, maple, or fruit.

Chocolate Marguerites

⅓ cup sifted Swans Down Cake Flour
¼ teaspoon soda
¼ teaspoon salt
½ cup brown sugar, firmly packed
2 eggs, well beaten
2 tablespoons butter or other shortening
1 square Baker's Unsweetened Chocolate, melted
2 tablespoons milk
½ teaspoon vanilla
1 cup chopped pecan meats

• Sift flour once, measure, add soda and salt, and sift together three times. Beat sugar gradually into beaten eggs. Melt shortening with chocolate and add to egg mixture; blend. Add milk and vanilla; then add flour and stir in quickly and thoroughly. Add nuts. Turn into greased small fancy pans. Place pecan half on each cake. Bake in moderate oven (375° F.) 10 minutes. Makes 2 dozen marguerites.

Chocolate Coconut Snowballs

• Use recipe for Devil's Food Cake (page 16). Spoon the batter into paper baking cups, set in muffin pans. Or spoon into muffin pans, greased on bottoms only, filling half full. Bake in moderate oven (350° F.) 15 to 20 minutes, or until done. Cool. Cover each cake with Fluffy Seven Minute Frosting (on page 73) and roll in Baker's Coconut. Makes 2½ dozen.

Oriole Devil's Food Cakes

• Use recipe for Devil's Food Cake (page 16). Spoon the batter into paper baking cups, set in muffin pans. Or spoon into muffin pans, greased on bottoms only, filling half full. Bake in moderate oven (350° F.) 15 to 20 minutes. Cool and spread tops with Orange Cream Cheese Frosting (page 77), tinted, or with Seven Minute Frosting (page 73, half recipe), flavored with lemon extract and tinted yellow. Makes 2½ dozen.

Looks like fairy-land magic, but, no, it's easy as pie to make this cloud-light filling and crisp Coconut Crust. See Pixie Pie, page 49.

Pie, A Universal Favorite

Make the men happy—with pie. Set a beautiful pie on the table with plenty of rich, velvety-smooth chocolate filling encased in tender flaky pastry and topped with golden brown mountains of meringue—is there any man who won't rise up and call you blessed? And as for the family, such a pie makes them charitable about even the most slender meal.

Just such a recipe is included in this section, called Velvet Chocolate Cream Pie. Use your favorite pastry recipe or try the easy-to-do Vanilla Wafer Crust. And you won't want to miss Chocolate Fudge Crust. It's an unexpected taste treat for family and guests.

Chocolate Meringue Pie

½ cup sugar (or ⅓ cup honey)
½ cup flour
½ teaspoon salt
2 ½ cups milk
2 squares Baker's Unsweetened Chocolate
3 egg yolks, slightly beaten
2 teaspoons butter
2 teaspoons vanilla
1 baked 9-inch pie shell

3 egg whites
6 tablespoons sugar

• Combine sugar, flour, and salt in top of double boiler, mixing very thoroughly. Add milk gradually, stirring well. Add chocolate. Place over boiling water and cook until chocolate is melted and mixture is thick and well blended, stirring constantly. Then continue cooking 10 minutes, stirring occasionally. Pour small amount of mixture over egg yolks, stirring vigorously; return to double boiler and cook 2 minutes longer. Add butter and vanilla. Cool. Turn into pie shell.

Beat egg whites until foamy throughout; add sugar, 2 tablespoons at a time, beating after each addition until sugar is blended. Then continue beating until mixture will stand in peaks. Pile lightly on filling. Bake in moderate oven (350° F.) 15 minutes, or until the meringue is delicately browned.

Baked Chocolate Custard

2 squares Baker's Unsweetened Chocolate
4 cups milk
4 eggs, slightly beaten
⅓ cup sugar
¼ teaspoon salt
1 teaspoon vanilla

• Add chocolate to milk and heat in double boiler. When chocolate is melted, beat with rotary egg beater until blended. Combine eggs, sugar, and salt; add chocolate mixture gradually, stirring until sugar is dissolved. Add vanilla and pour into custard cups. Place in pan of hot water and bake in slow oven (325° F.) 45 minutes, or until knife inserted comes out clean. (Water in pan should not reach boiling temperature.) Chill. Top with cream and a dash of cinnamon, or unmold and serve with cream, if desired. Serves 8 to 10.

You'll taste fame with Chocolate Icebox Cake. It's a masterpiece-dessert, right for any occasion. Choose one on page 57 or page 98.

Chocolate Custard Sponge Pudding

2 squares Baker's Unsweetened Chocolate
2 cups milk
4 tablespoons flour
½ cup sugar
¼ teaspoon salt
2 tablespoons melted butter
3 egg yolks, slightly beaten
1½ teaspoons vanilla
3 egg whites

• Add chocolate to milk and heat in double boiler. When chocolate is melted, beat with rotary egg beater until blended. Combine flour, sugar, and salt. Add butter and mix well; then add egg yolks. Add hot chocolate mixture gradually, blending thoroughly. Add vanilla. Beat egg whites until they will stand in soft peaks; then stir gently into chocolate mixture. Turn into greased 8-inch round baking dish. Place in pan of hot water and bake in moderate oven (350° F.) 45 to 50 minutes. Serve warm or cold, with cream. Serves 6 to 8.

Chocolate Tapioca Cream

1 egg white
2 tablespoons sugar
1 egg yolk
2 cups milk
⅓ cup sugar
⅛ teaspoon salt
2 tablespoons Minute Tapioca
1 square Baker's Unsweetened Chocolate
½ teaspoon vanilla

• Beat egg white until foamy throughout; add 2 tablespoons sugar, 1 at a time, and continue beating with rotary egg beater until mixture stands in very soft peaks. Set aside.

Mix egg yolk with a small amount of the milk in saucepan. Add ⅓ cup sugar, salt, Minute Tapioca, remaining milk, and chocolate. Place over medium heat. Cook until mixture comes to a boil, stirring constantly—5 to 8 minutes. (Do not overcook . . . mixture thickens as it cools.) Pour small amount of hot mixture gradually on egg-white meringue; blend. Add remaining mixture, stirring constantly. Add vanilla. Cool, stirring once after 15 to 20 minutes. Chill. Serves 4 or 5.

Chocolate Custard Bread Pudding

2 squares Baker's Unsweetened Chocolate
2¼ cups milk
2 eggs
½ cup sugar
¼ teaspoon salt
1 teaspoon vanilla
2 cups cubed stale bread

• Add chocolate to milk and heat in double boiler. When chocolate is melted, stir until blended. Beat eggs until foamy; add sugar and salt. Then add chocolate mixture gradually, stirring vigorously. Add vanilla. Place bread in greased baking dish; pour mixture over it and let stand 5 minutes. Mix well before baking. Place dish in pan of hot water and bake in moderate oven (350° F.) 50 minutes, or until pudding is firm. Serve warm or cold with cream. Serves 6.

Chocolate Soufflé

2 squares Baker's Unsweetened Chocolate
1½ cups milk
½ cup sugar
⅓ cup flour
½ teaspoon salt
2 tablespoons butter
1 teaspoon vanilla
4 egg yolks, beaten until thick and lemon-colored
4 egg whites, stiffly beaten

• Add chocolate to milk and heat in double boiler. When chocolate is melted, beat with rotary egg beater until blended. Combine sugar, flour, and salt; add small amount of chocolate mixture, stirring until smooth; return to double boiler and cook until thickened, stirring constantly; then continue cooking 5 minutes, stirring occasionally. Add butter and vanilla; cool slightly while beating eggs. Add egg yolks and mix well. Fold into egg whites. Turn into greased baking dish. Place in pan of hot water and bake in moderate oven (375° F.) 50 minutes, or until soufflé is firm. Serve immediately with Chocolate Mint Sauce (page 83) or with cream. Serves 8.

The baking dish may first be buttered and dusted with granulated sugar to give interesting finish and texture.

Brownie Pudding

½ cup sifted flour
1 teaspoon Calumet Baking Powder
½ teaspoon salt
⅓ cup granulated sugar
1 tablespoon Baker's Cocoa
¼ cup milk
1 tablespoon shortening, melted
½ teaspoon vanilla
¼ cup chopped nuts, if desired

½ cup firmly packed brown sugar
2 tablespoons Baker's Cocoa
¾ cup boiling water

• Sift flour once, measure, add baking powder, salt, granulated sugar, and 1 tablespoon cocoa, and sift again. Add milk, shortening, and vanilla; mix only until smooth. Then add nuts. Pour into greased casserole or small baking dish.

Mix together brown sugar and 2 tablespoons cocoa; sprinkle over batter. Then pour boiling water over top of the batter. (This makes a chocolate sauce in the bottom of pan after pudding is baked.) Bake in moderate oven (350° F.) 30 to 40 minutes. Makes 6 to 8 servings.

Chocolate Meringue Pudding

• Use Chocolate Pudding (below). Pour into greased baking dish. Top with meringue made with 2 egg whites and 4 tablespoons sugar. Bake in hot oven (425° F.) 5 minutes.

Chocolate Pudding

¾ cup sugar
5 tablespoons flour
¼ teaspoon salt
3 cups milk
3 squares Baker's Unsweetened Chocolate
1 teaspoon vanilla

• Combine sugar, flour, and salt in top of double boiler, mixing very thoroughly. Add milk gradually, stirring well. Add chocolate. Place over boiling water and cook and stir until thickened; then continue cooking 10 minutes, stirring occasionally. Add vanilla. Chill and serve with cream. Serves 6.

Chocolate Pudding Variations

• Chocolate Pudding (above) may be varied in many simple ways by the addition of other ingredients as listed here. These will suggest still other variations.

Fold ½ cup Baker's Premium Shred Coconut (plain or toasted) into pudding; top with additional coconut.

Fold ½ cup chopped walnut meats into pudding; top with a sprinkling of nuts or a walnut half.

Fold 1 diced banana into pudding; top with a few banana slices or with ring of banana slices.

Fold orange marmalade into whipped cream; use as garnish for pudding, topping with a bit of marmalade.

Fold a few slices of dates into pudding; top with date slices. Diced figs may be used in this way.

Flavor whipped cream garnish with peppermint extract. Top with sprig of mint or cube of mint jelly.

Umm! Old-fashioned Chocolate Pudding. How long since you treated your family to this old-time favorite? The recipe is right here.

Chocolate Fruit Pudding

2 cups sifted flour
2 teaspoons Calumet Baking Powder
½ teaspoon soda
¼ teaspoon salt
⅓ cup butter or other shortening
1 cup sugar
1 egg, slightly beaten
3 squares Baker's Unsweetened Chocolate, melted
1 cup milk
1 cup chopped raisins
1 teaspoon grated orange rind

• Sift flour once, measure, add baking powder, soda, and salt, and sift together three times. Cream shortening, add sugar gradually, and cream together thoroughly. Add egg and chocolate, beating until smooth. Add flour, alternately with milk, a small amount at a time, beating well after each addition. Fold in raisins and orange rind.

Turn into one greased 2-quart mold or two 1-quart molds. Cover tightly and steam 1¾ to 2 hours, depending on size of mold. Or turn into greased 2-quart casserole or 9-inch tube pan. Cover with greased brown or heavy waxed paper and tie securely. Place in pan of hot water and bake in moderate oven (375° F.) 2 hours, or until done. Serve hot with Sunshine Foamy Sauce (page 83), or with a simple orange sauce or raisin sauce, or with cream. Serves 10.

Chocolate Dessert Waffles

1½ cups sifted Swans Down Cake Flour
1½ teaspoons Calumet Baking Powder
½ teaspoon salt
½ cup sugar
2 egg yolks, well beaten
¾ cup milk
½ cup melted butter or other shortening
2 squares Baker's Unsweetened Chocolate, melted
½ teaspoon vanilla
2 egg whites

• Sift flour once, measure, add baking powder, salt, and sugar, and sift again. Combine egg yolks and milk; add to flour mixture, beating until smooth. Combine butter and chocolate; add to batter and blend. Add vanilla. Beat egg whites until they will hold up in moist peaks. Stir quickly but thoroughly into batter. Bake in hot waffle iron. Serve hot with vanilla or other ice cream and Regal Chocolate Sauce (page 82) or Log Cabin Syrup. Or soften orange marmalade by stirring well and use as sauce for waffles. May also be served with Cherry Sauce (page 82) or a simple orange sauce. Makes 5 waffles.

Note: Waffles may be made in advance. Before serving, reheat in oven just until hot and crisp.

Luscious Chocolate Icebox Cake

- 3 squares Baker's Unsweetened Chocolate
- ½ cup sugar
- Dash of salt
- ¼ cup hot water
- 1 tablespoon cold water
- 1½ teaspoons granulated gelatin
- 4 egg yolks
- 1 teaspoon vanilla
- 4 egg whites, stiffly beaten
- ½ cup cream, whipped
- 2 dozen lady fingers

• Melt chocolate in top of double boiler. Add sugar, salt, and hot water, stirring until sugar is dissolved and mixture blended. Add cold water to gelatin and mix. Add to hot chocolate mixture and stir until gelatin is dissolved; then cook until mixture is smooth and well thickened. Remove from boiling water; add egg yolks, one at a time, beating thoroughly after each. Place over boiling water and cook 2 minutes, stirring constantly. Add vanilla; cool. Fold into egg whites. Chill. Fold in whipped cream.

Line bottom and sides of mold with waxed paper. Arrange lady fingers on bottom and sides of mold. Add thin layer of thickened chocolate mixture, then arrange lady fingers and chocolate mixture in alternate layers, topping with chocolate mixture. Cut off lady fingers around sides of mold and arrange cut pieces on chocolate mixture. Chill 12 to 24 hours in refrigerator. Unmold. Serves 8 to 10.

If desired, ½ cup finely cut walnut meats may be added to chocolate mixture before turning into mold. Toast nuts lightly by heating and stirring with a little butter or oil.

Chocolate Thrift Pudding

1 square Baker's Unsweetened Chocolate
1/3 cup milk
1/3 cup sugar
Dash of salt
1/2 teaspoon Calumet Baking Powder
2 cups fine soft bread crumbs
1 teaspoon vanilla
1 egg, beaten until thick and fluffy

• Add chocolate to milk and place over low flame. Cook until mixture is smooth and blended, stirring constantly. Add sugar and salt and stir until sugar is dissolved. Remove from fire; add baking powder, bread crumbs, and vanilla; mix well. Then add egg and mix lightly. Turn into custard cups; bake in moderate oven (350°F.) 25 minutes. Serves 5.

Cocoa Rice Pudding

4 tablespoons rice
4 cups milk
1/2 teaspoon salt
1/2 cup sugar
1/2 teaspoon cinnamon
4 tablespoons Baker's Cocoa

• Wash rice thoroughly and combine with milk and salt in greased deep baking dish. Bake in slow oven (300° F.) 2 to 2 1/2 hours, or until creamy, stirring occasionally. Combine sugar, cinnamon, and cocoa, and stir into rice. Bake 15 minutes longer. Serve warm or cold with cream. Serves 6.

Chocolate Grape-Nuts Puff

4 tablespoons butter
1/2 cup sugar
2 egg yolks, well beaten
1 square Baker's Unsweetened Chocolate, melted
2 tablespoons flour
4 tablespoons Grape-Nuts
1 cup milk
2 egg whites, stiffly beaten

• Cream butter; add sugar gradually, blending after each addition. Add egg yolks and beat thoroughly; then add melted chocolate and blend. Add flour, Grape-Nuts, and milk, mixing well. Fold in egg whites. Turn into greased baking dish and place in pan of hot water. Bake in slow oven (325° F.) 1 hour and 15 minutes. Serve cold with cream. Serves 6.

Economy Chocolate Ice Cream

- 2 squares Baker's Unsweetened Chocolate
- 1 can (14 or 15 ounces) sweetened condensed milk
- Dash of salt
- 1 cup water
- ½ teaspoon vanilla
- ½ cup cream, whipped

• Melt chocolate in top of double boiler. Add condensed milk and salt and blend. Cook over rapidly boiling water 5 minutes, stirring constantly. Add water gradually, stirring constantly. Chill. Add vanilla. Fold chocolate mixture into whipped cream. Turn into freezing tray of automatic refrigerator and freeze. When mixture is frozen on sides and bottom, turn into chilled bowl and beat with rotary egg beater until smooth and increased in volume. Return to freezing tray and freeze 2 to 3 hours longer, or until firm. Makes about ¾ quart ice cream.

Regal Chocolate Mousse

- 3 squares Baker's Unsweetened Chocolate
- ⅓ cup water
- ¾ cup sugar
- ⅛ teaspoon salt
- 3 egg yolks, well beaten
- 1 teaspoon vanilla
- 2 cups cream, whipped

• Combine chocolate and water in saucepan. Bring to a boil over low flame, stirring vigorously until blended. Add sugar and salt and simmer 3 minutes, stirring constantly. Pour slowly over egg yolks, stirring well. Cool. Add vanilla and fold in whipped cream. Turn into freezing tray of automatic refrigerator and freeze 3 to 4 hours. Or turn mixture into mold, filling it to overflowing; cover with waxed paper and press cover tightly down over paper. Pack in equal parts ice and salt 3 to 4 hours. Serves 8 to 10. To vary, add ½ cup macaroon crumbs and ½ teaspoon almond extract before freezing.

Chocolate Velvet Cream

2 squares Baker's Unsweetened Chocolate
1 tablespoon granulated gelatin
¼ cup cold milk
1¼ cups milk, scalded
½ cup sugar
⅛ teaspoon salt
1 cup heavy cream
¾ teaspoon vanilla

• Melt chocolate in top of double boiler. Soak gelatin in ¼ cup milk 5 minutes. Add scalded milk, sugar, and salt and stir until gelatin is dissolved; add cream. Pour gelatin mixture slowly into melted chocolate, beating with rotary egg beater until blended; then cook 5 minutes. Remove from boiling water and add vanilla. Chill until cold and syrupy. Place in bowl of cracked ice or ice water and whip with rotary egg beater until thickened. Turn into mold. Chill until firm. Serve plain or with whipped cream. Serves 6.

This pudding may also be molded in individual molds or turned into sherbet glasses.

Chocolate Mint Cream

• Use recipe for Chocolate Velvet Cream (above). Dissolve gelatin as directed. Add only 2 cups gelatin mixture to melted chocolate. Pour ½ of chocolate mixture into large mold or individual molds and chill until firm. Place remaining chocolate mixture over lukewarm water until ready to mold.

To the remaining plain gelatin mixture, add few drops peppermint extract and green coloring to tint a delicate green. Chill until cold and syrupy. Place in bowl of cracked ice or ice water and whip with rotary egg beater until thickened. Turn into mold over firm chocolate layer and chill until firm. Top with remaining chocolate mixture. Chill until firm. Serve plain or with whipped cream.

Chocolate Frozen Pudding

• Use recipe for Delicious Chocolate Ice Cream (below). Fold ½ cup each finely cut raisins and figs into mixture before turning into tray or mold. Stir after freezing 45 minutes.

Nut meats may be substituted for either fruit. If desired, ¾ teaspoon rum extract may be added.

Delicious Chocolate Ice Cream

1 ½ squares Baker's Unsweetened Chocolate
⅓ cup sugar
Dash of salt
1 cup milk
3 egg yolks, slightly beaten
1 teaspoon vanilla
1 cup cream, whipped

• Add chocolate, sugar, and salt to milk and heat in double boiler. When chocolate is melted, beat with rotary egg beater until blended. Pour small amount of mixture over egg yolks, stirring vigorously; return to double boiler and cook 2 minutes longer, stirring constantly. Chill.

Fold chocolate mixture and vanilla into whipped cream. Turn into freezing tray of automatic refrigerator and let stand 3 to 4 hours. Or turn mixture into mold, filling it to overflowing; cover with waxed paper and press cover down tightly. Pack in equal parts ice and salt 4 hours. Makes about ¾ quart.

Note: Two eggs may be substituted for 3 egg yolks in above recipe. Add egg yolks as directed above. Fold stiffly beaten whites into chilled chocolate before folding into cream.

Old-fashioned Chocolate Ice Cream

1 cup sugar
4 tablespoons flour
⅛ teaspoon salt
2 cups milk
3 squares Baker's Unsweetened Chocolate
2 eggs, slightly beaten
4 cups light cream
2 tablespoons vanilla

• Combine sugar, flour, and salt in top of double boiler, mixing very thoroughly. Add milk gradually, stirring well. Add chocolate. Place over boiling water and cook and stir until thickened; then continue cooking 10 minutes, stirring occasionally. Pour small amount of mixture over eggs, stirring vigorously; return to double boiler and cook 2 minutes longer. Cool. Add cream and vanilla. Freeze until stiff, using 8 parts ice to 1 part salt. Remove dasher and cover tightly; repack in 4 parts ice to 1 part salt. Makes 2 quarts ice cream.

Candies Made at Home

Most of us with a sweet tooth love the making as well as the tasting of fine homemade candies. We like to surprise folks with a box of our own wonderful fudge, or treat them to our best chewy caramels.

Here's where Baker's Chocolate steps in with a special selection of recipes—excellent ones for such favorites. You'll find many more in other sections of this book, especially on pages 94 and 100 to 107.

SOME HELPFUL SUGGESTIONS

There are two main classes of candies: (1) *creamy or soft;* (2) *chewy or hard.* The difference is mainly in the temperature to which they are cooked. In creamy candies, we have a mass of tiny sugar crystals, suspended in a sugar syrup. In making hard or chewy candies, the temperature is so high that the sugar changes its form and becomes a clear, hard mass upon cooling—unless large amounts of corn syrup, milk, or cream are added, making the candy chewy instead.

Fudge and fondant are good examples of creamy candies. Caramels and brittles are chewy or hard candies.

When making either kind of candy, be sure that the sugar is completely dissolved during cooking and that the candy is taken from the heat at the right temperature. A candy thermometer is the surest guide.

For creamy candies, the mixture is cooled to lukewarm (110° F.) before beating or stirring in any way. This gives smaller, finer crystals which are not even noticed when the candy is eaten. For chewy or hard candies, pour mixture into greased pans immediately after removing from heat. Do not scrape the pan—this is likely to produce grainy streaks and give an unpleasant texture.

In this section is a recipe for Chocolate Fondant. It has many possibilities for variation. Make some of it into centers—either plain or with nuts or with Baker's Coconut—and dip them in Baker's Dot Chocolate. It's the ideal chocolate for dipping.

Chocolate Fudge

2 squares Baker's Unsweetened Chocolate
¾ cup milk
2 cups sugar
Dash of salt
2 tablespoons butter
1 teaspoon vanilla

• Add chocolate to milk and place over low flame. Cook until mixture is smooth and blended, stirring constantly. Add sugar and salt, and stir until sugar is dissolved and mixture boils. Continue boiling, without stirring, until a small amount of mixture forms a very soft ball in cold water (232° F.). Remove from fire. Add butter and vanilla. Cool to lukewarm (110° F.); then beat until mixture begins to thicken and loses its gloss. Turn at once into greased pan, 8x4 inches. When cold, cut in squares. Makes 18 large pieces.

No gift could be more welcome than smooth rich Fudge. Vary with marshmallows, nuts, raisins, candied fruits, as suggested on page 64.

Reliance Fudge

• Use recipe for Chocolate Fudge (page 63), adding 1 tablespoon corn syrup with sugar. Boil candy to 234° F. The addition of corn syrup requires a higher temperature. Cool and beat as directed.

Chocolate Nut or Raisin Fudge

• Use recipe for Chocolate Fudge (page 63) or Reliance Fudge (above). Add 1 cup broken nut meats or 1 cup seedless raisins just before turning into pan.

Marshmallow Fudge

• Use recipe for Chocolate Fudge (page 63). Cut 16 marshmallows (4 ounces) in halves; arrange in greased pan, 8x4 inches, placing cut-side up. Pour beaten fudge over marshmallows.

Tutti-frutti Fudge

• Use recipe for Chocolate Fudge (page 63), adding chopped candied or dried fruits and nuts before turning into pan. Some of fruit mixture may be sprinkled on top of fudge. For fruit, use about ¼ cup each candied cherries, candied pineapple, figs, and raisins. Wash, dry thoroughly, and cut fine. Add ¼ cup chopped, blanched pistachios or other nuts.

Cocoa Fudge

6 tablespoons Baker's Cocoa
2 cups sugar
Dash of salt
⅔ cup water or milk
2 tablespoons butter
1 teaspoon vanilla

• Combine cocoa, sugar, salt, water, butter. Cook over low heat until mixture boils, stirring constantly. Cover pan for 3 minutes. Remove cover and continue boiling, without stirring, until a small amount of mixture forms a soft ball in cold water (234° F.). Remove from heat. Add the vanilla and cool to lukewarm (110° F.). Beat until mixture just begins to thicken and loses its gloss. Spread at once in greased pan, 9x5 inches. When firm, cut in squares. Makes 24 pieces.

Chocolate Fondant

2 cups sugar
Dash of salt
1 1/4 cups water
2 tablespoons light corn syrup
2 tablespoons butter
1 teaspoon vanilla
3 squares Baker's Unsweetened Chocolate, melted

• Combine sugar, salt, water, corn syrup. Place over low heat and stir constantly until sugar is dissolved and mixture boils. Cover and cook 3 minutes; then remove cover and continue boiling, without stirring, until a small amount of syrup forms a soft ball in cold water (238° F.). Wash down sides of pan occasionally with damp cloth. Add butter. Pour out on cold, wet platter or porcelain table top, or on greased surface. Cool to lukewarm (110° F.). Work with paddle or spatula until white and creamy. Add vanilla and knead until smooth.

Shape in ball; make indentation in top and pour about 1/4 of chocolate into it. Knead until chocolate is blended. Repeat until all chocolate is used. Store in tightly covered jar to ripen for several days before using. If fondant begins to dry out, cover with damp cloth. Makes 1 pound 2½ ounces candy.

Chocolate Nut Patties

• Use recipe for Chocolate Fondant (above). Shape in small balls; flatten balls slightly and press half walnut meat into each. Makes 3 dozen 1-inch patties.

Chocolate Balls

• Use recipe for Chocolate Fondant (above), adding 1 cup finely cut raisins. Shape in small balls. Roll in chopped nuts or toasted Baker's Coconut. Makes 6 dozen balls.

Chocolate Slices

• Use recipe for Chocolate Fondant (above), adding ¾ cup finely cut dates or raisins, and ¾ cup nut meats, finely cut, or Baker's Coconut. Knead and shape in rolls, 1 inch in diameter. Wrap in waxed paper and chill. When firm, cut in ¼-inch slices. Makes 1¾ pounds candy, or six 8-inch rolls.

Chocolate Caramels

1 cup sugar
¾ cup corn syrup
3 squares Baker's Unsweetened Chocolate
¼ teaspoon salt
1½ cups light cream

• Combine sugar, corn syrup, chocolate, salt, and ½ cup cream. Place over low flame and stir constantly until sugar is dissolved and mixture boils. Continue boiling until a small amount of mixture forms a soft ball in cold water (234° F.), stirring constantly. Add ½ cup cream and boil again to 234° F., stirring constantly. Add remaining ½ cup cream and boil slowly until a small amount of mixture forms a firm ball in cold water (242° F.), stirring constantly. Pour into slightly buttered pan, 8x4 inches. Do not scrape pan. Let stand until cold.

Mark with knife in ¾-inch squares and turn out on cold slab, turning top-side up. Cut in squares, using full length of long blade. Let stand in cool place to dry. Makes 40.

Chocolate Nut Caramels

• Use recipe for Chocolate Caramels (above). Add 1 cup broken nut meats just before pouring mixture into pan.

If you want smooth, creamy fudge, watch for this turning point. The mixture thickens, loses gloss . . . It's time to pour. Recipe, page 63.

Hot Chocolate—A Traditional Drink

The first known use of chocolate was as a beverage. When the Spanish first came to the New World, they discovered that the Mexican Indians were consuming vast quantities of a savory food-drink which they called "chocolatl." This exciting new beverage was quickly introduced into Spain and immediately found favor there. According to one old recipe, here is the way they prepared it in those days:

> "Take a hundred cacao Kernels, two heads of Chili or long peppers, a handful of anise or orjevala, and two of mesachusil or vanilla,—or instead six Alexandria roses, powdered—two drachmas of cinnamon, a dozen almonds, and as many hazel nuts, a half a pound of white sugar, and anette enough to color it, and you have the king of chocolates."

Little would you imagine that our present day easy-to-prepare recipe for steaming, fragrant hot chocolate evolved from such a spicy, intricate mixture!

Chocolate is more than just something good to drink. It's a food that supplies real nourishment. It combines so beautifully in beverages with eggs and milk that a chocolate drink can make up the main part of a simple meal.

What is more refreshing and nourishing on a hot day than a tall, frosty Chocolate Float! This can be made at a moment's notice if you have a place reserved in your refrigerator for Premium Chocolate Syrup or Cocoa Syrup—whichever you prefer. For that extra cool touch, flavor your iced chocolate with a bit of peppermint extract and garnish with a fresh sprig of mint.

WHEN YOU ENTERTAIN

The French Chocolate, which looks as luscious as it tastes, may also be prepared ahead of time. All you have to do before serving is to heat the milk. Spooned into slender chocolate cups as the hot milk is poured from a dignified chocolate pot, you have an unusual and charming service to distinguish this favorite party drink.

The chocolate mixture used for preparing French Chocolate is delectable as a sauce, too, with or without the whipped cream. So it pays to keep some on hand.

A CHOCOLATE SECRET

Long, slow cooking brings out extra smoothness and richer chocolate flavor. Make your hot chocolate ahead of time and leave it over boiling water, covered, to season and mellow in flavor. You can forget about it for an extra half or three-quarters of an hour. Then beat up all nice and foamy, serve, and listen to the applause!

Premium Chocolate Syrup

3 squares Baker's Unsweetened Chocolate
2/3 cup water
1/2 cup sugar
Dash of salt
1/2 cup corn syrup
1/2 teaspoon vanilla

• Place chocolate and water in saucepan. Cook slowly until thick and well blended, stirring constantly. Add sugar and salt; bring to a boil and boil gently 2 minutes, stirring constantly. (For a thicker sauce, boil 4 minutes.) Add corn syrup and bring again to a boil. Remove from heat. Cool slightly, then add vanilla. Turn into jar; cover tightly. Keep in refrigerator. Makes about 1 1/2 cups syrup. Serve hot or cold as sauce or use in chocolate drinks.

For chocolate drinks, use 2 tablespoons syrup to 1 cup milk.

Cocoa Syrup

1 cup Baker's Cocoa
2/3 cup sugar
2/3 cup corn syrup
1/4 teaspoon salt
1 cup cold water
1/2 teaspoon vanilla

• Combine cocoa, sugar, syrup, and salt in saucepan. Add water slowly and place over low heat, stirring until smooth;

then boil gently 3 minutes, stirring constantly. Add vanilla. Turn into jar; cover tightly. Keep in refrigerator. Makes about 2 cups syrup. Serve hot or cold as sauce or use in making delicious cocoa drinks. (To make without the corn syrup, increase sugar to 1¼ cups and use ¼ cup more water.)

To make cold drinks, use 2 tablespoons syrup to 1 cup milk.

Chocolate Milk Shake

1 cup chilled milk
2 tablespoons Premium Chocolate Syrup
or Cocoa Syrup (above)

• Add milk slowly to syrup, stirring constantly. Beat or shake well. Pour into tall glass and serve at once. Serves 1.

Evaporated Milk Shake

• Substitute ½ cup evaporated milk and ¼ cup water for chilled milk in Chocolate Milk Shake (above). Add to syrup and shake with cracked ice until foamy. Serves 1.

Chocolate Malted Milk

2 tablespoons malted milk powder
2 tablespoons Premium Chocolate Syrup
or Cocoa Syrup (above)
1 cup chilled milk

• Add malted milk powder to syrup, stirring until smooth and thoroughly blended. Add milk slowly, stirring constantly. Beat or shake well. Pour into tall glass and serve at once. Serves 1.

Chocolate Ice Cream Soda

½ cup chilled milk
2 tablespoons Premium Chocolate Syrup
or Cocoa Syrup (above)
½ cup carbonated water
Chocolate or vanilla ice cream

• Add milk slowly to syrup, stirring constantly; pour into tall glass. Add carbonated water and stir enough to mix. Add ice cream and serve at once. Serves 1.

Chocolate Eggnog

1 cup chilled milk
3 tablespoons Premium Chocolate Syrup
or Cocoa Syrup (page 68)
1 egg, well beaten

• Add milk slowly to syrup, stirring constantly; add to egg, and beat or shake well. Pour into tall glass; serve. Serves 1.

Chocolate Float

1 cup chilled milk
2 tablespoons Premium Chocolate Syrup
or Cocoa Syrup (page 68)
Chocolate ice cream

• Add milk slowly to syrup, stirring constantly. Beat or shake well. Pour into tall glass. Add ice cream. Serves 1.

Hot Chocolate

2 squares Baker's Unsweetened Chocolate
1 cup water
3 tablespoons sugar
Dash of salt
3 cups milk

• Add chocolate to water in top of double boiler and place over low flame, stirring until chocolate is melted and blended. Add sugar and salt and boil 3 minutes, stirring constantly. Place over boiling water. Add milk gradually, stirring constantly; then heat. Just before serving, beat with rotary egg beater until light and frothy. Serves 6.

Iced Chocolate

• Use recipe for Hot Chocolate (above). Cool well so that ice will not dilute beverage. Pour over cracked ice in tall glasses. Stir well to blend and chill. Serves 4.

Brazilian Chocolate

• Use recipe for Hot Chocolate (above), substituting 1 cup strong coffee for water. Cook as directed. When hot, beat with rotary egg beater until light and frothy. Cool. Pour over ice in tall glasses. Serves 4.

French Chocolate

2 ½ squares Baker's Unsweetened Chocolate
½ cup water
½ cup sugar
Dash of salt
½ cup cream, whipped
6 cups hot milk

• Add chocolate to water and place over low flame, stirring until chocolate is melted and blended. Add sugar and salt and boil 4 minutes, stirring constantly. Cool. Fold into cream. Place 1 rounding teaspoon of chocolate mixture in each chocolate cup; add hot milk to fill cup and stir until chocolate and milk are well blended. Serves 18. For larger cups (6-ounce size), use 1 rounding tablespoon chocolate mixture. Serves 8.

This chocolate mixture also makes an excellent sauce. The whipped cream may be omitted and sauce served as hot fudge.

Quick tricks from one recipe are Chocolate Squares and Cookies. Change to suit your crowd for lunches or parties. Pages 38 and 39.

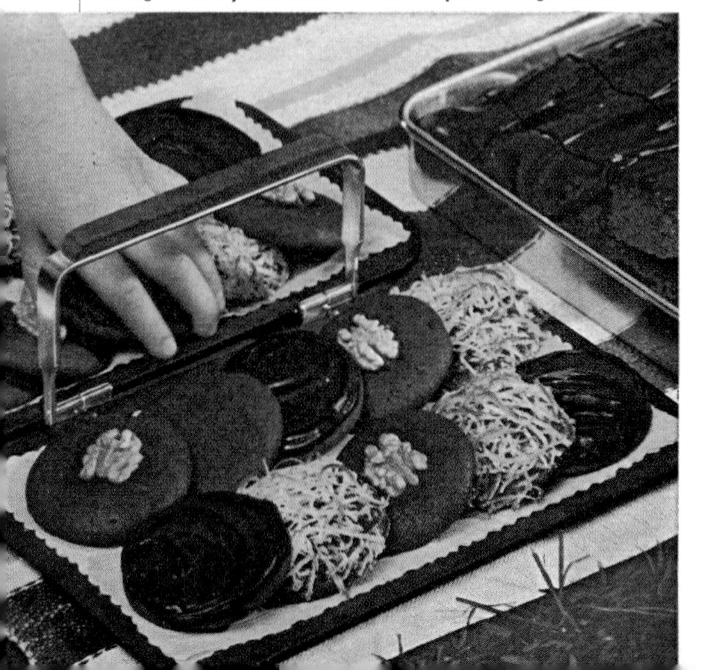

Distinctive Frostings

When that perfect frosting swirls over the cake, then you know that victory perches on your spatula! Choose from the satiny or fluffy frostings in this section and your cake will come to the table in a burst of hurrahs.

Popular Seven Minute Frosting is the lead-off choice followed with its interesting and good-flavor variations. These are handsome frostings to make handsome cakes of your deep rich chocolate layers.

For chocolate frostings, you can pick any kind—the simple uncooked, the cooked creamy fudge type, or rich Hungarian, using egg yolks. And remember, in chocolate frostings, you can use margarine instead of butter. There are favorite-flavor frostings to go with chocolate cakes, too—orange and coffee or Mocha.

FROSTING YOUR CAKE

Frosting a cake is an art. Some people are more gifted than others, but everyone can turn out a cake that is good to look at. Here are a few simple directions to follow.

1. Be sure that both cake and frosting are cool.
2. Brush off all loose crumbs and trim any ragged edges with scissors.
3. Frost sides of cake first, spreading lightly over the top edge and down around the sides in sweeping strokes.
4. Then fill in center top and work out to edges, making beautiful swirls or folds with your knife or spatula or the back of a silver spoon.
5. In frosting a layer cake, place bottom layer top-side down and spread frosting smoothly. Then place next layer on top, matching edges. Finish frosting as above.

WHEN THE SAUCE MAKES THE PUDDING

What surprises can be wrought in plain-jane pudding or ice cream by the addition of a delicious sauce! Here you will find an interesting collection. Select a sauce which does not cover the flavor of the dessert, but which accents it, blends with it, or adds needed richness.

Seven Minute Frosting

2 egg whites, unbeaten
1½ cups sugar
Dash of salt
⅓ cup water
2 teaspoons light corn syrup
1 teaspoon vanilla

• Combine egg whites, sugar, salt, water, and corn syrup in top of double boiler, beating with rotary egg beater until well mixed. Place over rapidly boiling water, beat constantly with rotary egg beater, and cook 7 minutes, or until frosting will stand in stiff peaks. Remove from boiling water; add vanilla. Beat until thick enough to spread. Makes enough frosting to cover tops and sides of two 9-inch layers, top and sides of three 9-inch layers, or tops and sides of three 8-inch layers.

For half-recipe, use 3 tablespoons water. Cook 4 minutes instead of 7. Makes frosting to cover top and sides of two 9-inch layers, or tops and sides of two 8-inch layers thinly.

Fluffy Seven Minute Frosting (All corn syrup)

2 egg whites, unbeaten
1½ cups light corn syrup
Dash of salt
1 teaspoon vanilla

• Cook as directed for Seven Minute Frosting (above). If frosting separates in the bottom of pan before spreading, beat with rotary egg beater until blended.

Almond Seven Minute Frosting

• Use recipe for Seven Minute Frosting or Fluffy Seven Minute Frosting (above), adding ½ teaspoon almond extract and decreasing vanilla to ¼ teaspoon.

Chocolate Seven Minute Frosting

• Use recipe for Seven Minute Frosting (above). Before spreading, add 2 or 3 squares Baker's Unsweetened Chocolate which have been melted and cooled; fold in chocolate gently but thoroughly. Do not beat mixture.

Mint Frosting

• Use recipe for Seven Minute Frosting or Fluffy Seven Minute Frosting (page 73), substituting ¼ teaspoon peppermint extract for vanilla. Add green coloring to hot frosting to give a delicate tint. Makes enough frosting for 15x10-inch roll. Or use on layer cake; cover with Chocolate Coating (page 80).

Peppermint Frosting

• Make as for Mint Frosting (above), adding red coloring instead of green to give frosting a delicate shell-pink tint. Spread on cake. While frosting is soft but cold, sprinkle chocolate flakes around top of cake to form 1-inch border.

For chocolate flakes, scrape chocolate with a sharp knife. Hold knife so that blade is at right angles to chocolate and scrape with a downward motion.

Cocoa Frosting

3 cups sifted confectioners' sugar
¼ teaspoon salt
¼ cup Baker's Cocoa
¼ cup butter
¼ cup hot milk
½ teaspoon vanilla

• Sift sugar, salt, and cocoa together. Cream butter until soft; add part of sugar mixture gradually, beating thoroughly. Add remaining sugar mixture, alternately with hot milk, beating well after each addition. Add vanilla. Makes enough frosting to cover tops of two 9-inch layers, or top and sides of 8x8x2-inch cake, or about 2 dozen cup cakes.

Quick Chocolate Frosting

2 squares Baker's Unsweetened Chocolate
1 can (14 or 15 ounces) sweetened condensed milk
1 tablespoon water
Dash of salt
½ teaspoon vanilla

• Melt chocolate in top of double boiler. Add condensed milk gradually, mixing well; then add water and salt and blend. Cook 5 minutes over rapidly boiling water, stirring constantly. Remove from fire. Add vanilla. Cool. Makes enough frosting to cover tops of two 9-inch layers, two 8-inch layers (generously), or top and sides of 8x8x2-inch cake or 9x5x3-inch loaf cake. Or enough to cover tops of 2 dozen medium cup cakes.

Note: Three squares Baker's Unsweetened Chocolate may be used for darker, richer flavored frosting. Increase water to 2 tablespoons and cook only 3 minutes.

Orange Chocolate Frosting

• Use recipe for Quick Chocolate Frosting (above). Add ¾ teaspoon grated orange rind after cooling frosting.

Quick Mocha Frosting

• Use recipe for Quick Chocolate Frosting (above). Substitute ¼ cup very strong coffee and ⅔ cup sweetened condensed milk for 1 can sweetened condensed milk. Makes enough frosting to cover tops of two 8-inch layers.

Glossy Hungarian Chocolate Frosting makes wonderful swirls. Frost top edge and sides first, then swirl more frosting over top. Page 76.

Hungarian Chocolate Frosting

4 to 5 squares Baker's Unsweetened Chocolate
2¼ cups sifted confectioners' sugar
¼ cup hot water
2 egg yolks or 1 whole egg, unbeaten
6 tablespoons butter, softened

• Melt chocolate over hot water. Remove from hot water, add sugar and ¼ cup hot water, and blend. Add egg yolks, one at a time, beating well after each. Add butter, 1 tablespoon at a time, beating until frosting is smooth. Makes 2 cups plus 2 tablespoons, or enough for tops and sides of two 9-inch layers, or top and sides of a 13x9x2-inch cake.

To make 1⅓ cups frosting, use 3 squares Baker's Unsweetened Chocolate, 1½ cups confectioners' sugar, 2 tablespoons hot water, 1 whole egg, and 4 tablespoons butter. Frosts 24 cupcakes, or top and sides of an 8-inch square cake.

Martha Washington Fudge Frosting

1½ cups sugar
¾ cup water
1 tablespoon corn syrup
Dash of salt
4 squares Baker's Unsweetened Chocolate
2 tablespoons butter
1 teaspoon vanilla

• Combine sugar, water, corn syrup, and salt in small saucepan. Bring quickly to a boil, stirring only until sugar is dissolved. Then boil, without stirring, until mixture forms a soft ball in cold water (234° F.). Cool slightly to 150° F. Melt chocolate in medium saucepan over boiling water. Add butter and vanilla. Remove from boiling water. Add syrup gradually, stirring constantly. Continue stirring until smooth and thickened. Place again over boiling water and stir until frosting is softened and of right consistency to spread. Remove from boiling water and spread on cake.

If necessary, place over hot water to keep soft while spreading, and if the frosting begins to lose its gloss, add 1 or 2 teaspoons of hot water and blend. Makes enough frosting to cover tops and sides of two 8x10-inch layers, or tops and sides of two 9-inch layers. Double this recipe for enough frosting to cover tops and sides of three 10-inch layers.

Cream Cheese Frosting

4 tablespoons butter
1½ packages (3-ounce size) cream cheese
½ teaspoon salt
3 cups sifted confectioners' sugar
1 tablespoon milk
½ teaspoon vanilla

• Cream butter, add cheese and salt, and blend. Add sugar, a small amount at a time, alternately with the milk, beating well after each addition. Add vanilla and blend. Makes enough frosting to cover tops of two 9-inch layers, tops and sides of two 8-inch layers, or top and sides of 9x9x2-inch cake.

Orange Cream Cheese Frosting

• Use recipe for Cream Cheese Frosting (above), adding 1 teaspoon grated orange rind to butter. Substitute 1 tablespoon orange juice for the milk.

Chocolate Sundae Frosting

4 squares Baker's Unsweetened Chocolate
3 cups sifted confectioners' sugar
4 tablespoons hot water
5 egg yolks
6 tablespoons softened butter
½ cup coarsely chopped nut meats

• Melt chocolate in double boiler. Remove from boiling water; add sugar and water and blend. Add egg yolks, one at a time, beating well after each. Add butter, a tablespoon at a time, beating thoroughly after each amount. Reserve ¼ cup frosting for decorating. Spread remaining frosting between layers and on top and sides of cake. Sprinkle nuts over top. Add 2 teaspoons hot water to reserved ¼ cup frosting. Place over hot water, stirring until thinned. Dribble over nuts. Makes enough to cover tops and sides of two 9-inch layers (generously).

Cherry Four Minute Frosting

• Use half-recipe for Seven Minute Frosting (page 73). Before spreading on cake, fold in 6 finely chopped maraschinos.

Clever Judy Mocha Frosting

1 cup sifted confectioners' sugar
1 egg, unbeaten
¼ cup strong coffee
½ teaspoon vanilla
3 squares Baker's Unsweetened Chocolate, melted
1 tablespoon softened butter

• Combine ingredients in order given, beating with rotary egg beater until blended. Place bowl in pan of cracked ice or ice water and continue beating until of right consistency to spread (about 3 minutes). Makes enough frosting to cover tops of two 9-inch layers, top and sides of 8x8x2-inch cake, top of 13x9x2-inch cake, or small angel food cake. For all-chocolate flavor, substitute milk for coffee.

Coffee-Chocolate Cream Frosting

1 package Jell-O Vanilla Pudding
1¼ cups strong coffee
⅓ cup milk
1 square Baker's Unsweetened Chocolate

• Place pudding powder in saucepan. Add liquids gradually, stirring constantly. Cook and stir over low heat until mixture comes to a boil and is thickened. Divide mixture in two parts; to one part add chocolate, stirring until blended. Cool both mixtures, stirring occasionally. Spread coffee frosting between two 8- or 9-inch layers and chocolate frosting on top.

Fudge Frosting

2 squares Baker's Unsweetened Chocolate
¾ cup milk
2 cups sugar
Dash of salt
2 teaspoons corn syrup
2 tablespoons butter
1 teaspoon vanilla

• Add chocolate to milk and place over low heat. Cook until mixture is smooth and blended, stirring constantly. Add sugar, salt, and corn syrup; stir until sugar is dissolved and mixture boils. Continue boiling, stirring occasionally, until a small amount forms a soft ball in cold water (232° F. to 234° F.). Remove from fire. Add butter and vanilla. Cool to lukewarm (110° F.). Beat until of right consistency to spread. If necessary, place over hot water to keep soft while spreading. Makes enough frosting to cover top and sides of 8x8x2-inch cake, tops and sides of two 8-inch layers, or tops of two 9-inch layers; or enough to cover tops of two 8x8-inch layers.

Bittersweet Chocolate Coating

3 squares Baker's Unsweetened Chocolate
⅓ cup sugar
4 tablespoons water

• Melt chocolate in small bowl over hot water; cool. Bring sugar and water to a boil and boil ½ minute. Cool until lukewarm. Add gradually to chocolate, stirring until blended. Cool, stirring occasionally. Makes enough frosting to cover tops of 16 bars, 4x1 inches, or 4 dozen tiny éclairs or cream puffs.

This lovely cake takes the prize for popularity with cooks. It's such a straightaway recipe . . . Golden Cream Chocolate Cake, page 28.

Chocolate Coating (To cover frosting)

2 squares Baker's Unsweetened Chocolate
2 teaspoons butter

• Melt chocolate and butter over hot water and blend. When frosting on cake is set, pour slightly cooled chocolate mixture from tip of spoon over cake, letting it run down on sides. Keep cake in cool place until chocolate is firm.

Raisin Filling

3 tablespoons Swans Down Cake Flour
⅓ cup sugar
1 tablespoon grated orange rind
¾ cup water
½ cup orange juice
2 cups seeded raisins, chopped

• Combine flour, sugar, and orange rind. Add water and orange juice, mixing well. Then add raisins and cook gently 5 minutes, or until thickened, stirring constantly. Cool to lukewarm. Makes 2⅓ cups filling, or enough to spread between three 9-inch layers.

Raisin Nut Filling

• Use recipe for Raisin Filling (above), increasing sugar to ½ cup. Add ⅔ cup chopped walnut or pecan meats to mixture before using. Or add ⅔ cup blanched almonds, toasted and chopped, for extra delicious flavor.

Golden Cream Filling

½ cup sugar
3 tablespoons Swans Down Cake Flour
¼ teaspoon salt
1½ cups milk
1 egg or 2 egg yolks, slightly beaten
½ teaspoon each vanilla and almond extract

• Combine sugar, flour, and salt in top of small double boiler; add the milk gradually, mixing thoroughly. Place over boiling water and cook 10 minutes, stirring constantly. Pour small amount over egg, stirring vigorously, return to double boiler; cook and stir 2 minutes. Cool; add flavoring. Makes 1⅔ cups.

Jell-O Butterscotch Cream Filling

1 package Jell-O Butterscotch Pudding
1 ¾ cups milk
½ cup cream, whipped

• Place pudding powder in saucepan. Add milk gradually, stirring constantly. Cook and stir over low flame until mixture comes to a boil and is thickened. Cool, stirring occasionally. Fold in whipped cream. Makes 2¼ cups filling.

Chocolate Cream Filling

1 ½ squares Baker's Unsweetened Chocolate
1 cup milk
6 tablespoons sugar
2 tablespoons Swans Down Cake Flour
¼ teaspoon salt
1 egg yolk, slightly beaten
½ tablespoon butter
½ teaspoon vanilla

• Add chocolate to milk and heat in double boiler. When chocolate is melted, beat with rotary egg beater until blended. Combine sugar, flour, and salt; add gradually to chocolate mixture and cook until thickened, stirring constantly; then continue cooking 10 minutes, stirring occasionally. Pour small amount of mixture over egg yolk, stirring vigorously; return to double boiler and cook 2 minutes longer, stirring constantly. Add butter and vanilla and cool. Makes 1¼ cups filling.

Whipped Cream Fruit Sauce

⅓ cup juice from canned fruit
1 teaspoon granulated gelatin
½ cup light cream
Dash of salt

• Mix juice with gelatin in small bowl. Heat and stir over boiling water until gelatin is dissolved. Remove from boiling water, add cream and salt, and mix. Place in bowl of ice and water and whip 5 to 7 minutes, or until mixture begins to set around edges. Remove from ice water; stir gently until smooth. Add sugar, if needed. Serve. Makes 1¼ cups.

How to Whip Light Cream

2 tablespoons cold water
1¼ teaspoons granulated gelatin
1 cup light cream
Few grains of salt

• Add water gradually to gelatin in small bowl, mixing well. Heat and stir over boiling water until gelatin is completely dissolved. Remove from boiling water, add cream and salt, and mix. Place in bowl of ice and water and whip at once with rotary egg beater 5 to 7 minutes, or until mixture begins to hold shape around side of bowl. Remove from ice water and stir gently with spoon until smooth. Serve; or store in refrigerator until needed, stirring well before using.

Or chill in refrigerator instead of ice. When thickened, beat until light and fluffy. Return to refrigerator to set slightly.

Cherry Sauce

½ cup sugar
2 tablespoons flour
¼ teaspoon salt
¾ cup cherry juice
¼ cup boiling water
2 teaspoons butter
1 cup pitted, canned red cherries, drained
2 tablespoons lemon juice

• Combine sugar, flour, and salt; add cherry juice and water, mixing thoroughly. Cook and stir over direct heat 5 minutes; add butter, cherries, lemon juice. Serve hot. Makes 2 cups.

Regal Chocolate Sauce

2 squares Baker's Unsweetened Chocolate
6 tablespoons water
½ cup sugar
Dash of salt
3 tablespoons butter
¼ teaspoon vanilla

• Add chocolate to water and place over low flame, stirring until blended. Add sugar and salt and cook until sugar is dissolved and mixture very slightly thickened, stirring constantly. Add butter and vanilla. Makes about 1 cup sauce.

Fluffy Chocolate Sauce

• Use recipe for Regal Chocolate Sauce (above). Fold ¼ cup sauce into ½ cup cream, whipped.

Chocolate Mint Sauce

• Use recipe for Regal Chocolate Sauce (above), adding ½ teaspoon mint extract with vanilla.

Chocolate Walnut Cream

4 tablespoons sugar
2 tablespoons flour
Dash of salt
¾ cup milk
1 square Baker's Unsweetened Chocolate
1 tablespoon butter
1 teaspoon vanilla
½ cup cream, whipped
½ cup chopped walnut meats

• Combine sugar, flour, and salt in top of double boiler. Add milk gradually, mixing thoroughly. Add chocolate. Cook over boiling water until thickened, stirring constantly. Then continue cooking 5 minutes, stirring occasionally. Add butter and vanilla; chill thoroughly. Fold in whipped cream and nuts. Makes 2 cups filling.

Sunshine Foamy Sauce

¼ cup brown sugar, firmly packed
1 egg yolk, unbeaten
Dash of salt
1 egg white, unbeaten
¼ cup cream, whipped
½ teaspoon vanilla

• Sift sugar. Add ½ of sugar to egg yolk and beat until light. Add salt to egg white and beat until foamy throughout. Add remaining sugar, 1 tablespoon at a time, beating after each addition until sugar is blended; then beat until stiff. Combine egg mixtures. Fold in whipped cream and vanilla. Or flavor with rum extract or sherry to taste. Makes 1⅓ cups sauce.

Recipes Made with Baker's Semi-Sweet Chocolate Chips

Here they are—exciting and popular chocolate chip recipes using Baker's Semi-Sweet Chocolate Chips. You'll love those rich, unexpected bits of chocolate which remain whole and crunchy even after baking!

This chocolate has taken the country by storm. There are requests for recipes from kitchens all over the land. People love the texture and delicious blend of bitter-sweet flavor they find in these dainty chocolate chips.

Baker's Semi-Sweet Chocolate Chips are all ready to use just as they come from the package. The family will love to eat them right out of the carton, but you, as the provider of extra-good-things at mealtime, will want to keep a special supply, hidden away, "for cooking only."

In this section you'll find all kinds of interesting recipes: Chocolate Chip Cookies and many other tempting cookies, cakes, puddings, and desserts; frostings, sauces, candies, and sweet chocolate spreads. If you miss any of them, you'll be sorry!

Most of these recipes call for adding Baker's Semi-Sweet Chocolate Chips right to the batter. This gives the delightful soft chip texture to the finished dish. However, some recipes call for melted chips. To melt, place chips in top of double boiler over hot or boiling water. Soon the chips will be melted and soft, even though they still hold shape. So stir to blend the melted mixture.

Chocolate Toastaroons

½ to 1 cup Baker's Semi-Sweet Chocolate Chips
5 cups Post Toasties
1 can (14 or 15 ounces) sweetened condensed milk

• Combine chocolate chips and Toasties. Add condensed milk, mixing lightly. Drop from teaspoon on greased baking sheet; flatten slightly, shaping edges with spoon. Bake in slow oven (325° F.) 12 to 15 minutes, or until done. Remove from baking sheet immediately, using knife or spatula. To keep cookies from sticking, hold pan over low flame a few seconds. Makes 40.

Chocolate Chip Cookies

1 cup plus 2 tablespoons sifted flour
½ teaspoon soda
½ teaspoon salt
½ cup granulated sugar
¼ cup firmly packed brown sugar
1 egg
½ cup soft butter or other shortening
1 teaspoon vanilla
½ cup chopped nuts
1 cup (6 ounces) Baker's Semi-Sweet Chocolate Chips

• Measure flour, add soda and salt, and sift into mixing bowl. Add sugars, egg, shortening, and vanilla. Blend; then mix thoroughly, about 1 minute. Stir in nuts and chocolate chips. Drop from teaspoon onto ungreased baking sheet, about 2 inches apart. Bake in moderate oven (375° F.) 10 to 12 minutes. Makes about 4 dozen cookies.

Chocolate Chip Cooky Bars

• Use recipe for Chocolate Chip Cookies (above). Spread the dough in ungreased 13x9x2-inch pan. Bake at 375° F. for 13 to 15 minutes. Cut at once into squares or rectangles. Makes about 4 dozen.

Chocolate Chip Macaroons

1 cup (6 ounces) Baker's Semi-Sweet Chocolate Chips
2 cups Baker's Coconut
½ teaspoon Calumet Baking Powder
¼ teaspoon salt
1 teaspoon vanilla
⅔ cup sweetened condensed milk

• Combine chocolate chips, coconut, baking powder, and salt. Add vanilla and condensed milk and mix well. Drop from teaspoon on lightly greased baking sheet and bake in slow oven (325° F.) 12 minutes, or until delicately browned. Makes about 2 dozen macaroons.

Note: One teaspoon grated orange rind may be added with vanilla. Or substitute ½ teaspoon peppermint extract for the vanilla if minted chocolate flavor is desired.

Chocolate Chip Queen Pudding

3 cups ½-inch cubes stale cake
¼ cup sugar
¼ teaspoon salt
2 egg yolks and 2 eggs
3 cups scalded milk
¾ teaspoon rum extract or 1 teaspoon vanilla
½ cup Baker's Semi-Sweet Chocolate Chips

2 egg whites
Dash of salt
4 tablespoons sugar

• Place cake cubes in greased 8½-inch casserole. Add ¼ cup sugar and ¼ teaspoon salt to eggs and beat slightly; then add milk and flavoring. Pour over cake and mix well. Place in pan of hot water and bake in moderate oven (350° F.) about 50 minutes, or until custard mixture is just set, not firm. Do not overbake at this stage.

Sprinkle chips over top and cover with meringue. To make meringue, beat egg whites with salt until foamy throughout. Then add 4 tablespoons sugar gradually, beating after each addition until sugar is blended; continue beating until mixture will stand in peaks. Return pudding to oven and bake 12 minutes, or until delicately browned. Serve warm. Serves 6.

Chocolate Chip Kisses

2 egg whites
⅛ teaspoon salt
⅛ teaspoon cream of tartar
½ cup sugar
1 cup (6 ounces) Baker's Semi-Sweet Chocolate Chips
½ teaspoon vanilla

• Beat egg whites until foamy throughout; then add salt and cream of tartar and continue beating until eggs are stiff enough to hold up in peaks, but not dry. Add sugar, 2 tablespoons at a time, beating thoroughly after each addition. Fold in chocolate chips and vanilla. Drop from teaspoon on ungreased heavy paper. Bake in slow oven (300° F.) 25 minutes, or until done. Remove from paper while slightly warm using a spatula. Makes about 36 chocolate kisses. May be varied by adding other ingredients and flavors as suggested below.

Chocolate Chip Peppermint Kisses

• Use recipe for Chocolate Chip Kisses (above). Substitute ¼ teaspoon peppermint extract for vanilla.

Chocolate Chip Toasties Kisses

• Use recipe for Chocolate Chip Kisses (above). Substitute ½ cup Baker's Semi-Sweet Chocolate Chips and 1½ cups Post Toasties for 1 cup chips. Makes 2 dozen. (One cup Grape-Nuts Flakes may be used instead of 1½ cups Post Toasties in making these kisses.)

Chocolate Chip Nut Kisses

• Use recipe for Chocolate Chip Kisses (above). Substitute ½ cup of Baker's Semi-Sweet Chocolate Chips and ½ cup chopped nut meats for 1 package chips.

Brownies, sure enough. But special, so your best beau or boy can see they're dressed up just for him. Make plenty! Recipe is on page 40.

Chocolate Chip Scotch Bars

1 cup sifted flour
½ teaspoon Calumet Baking Powder
⅛ teaspoon soda
½ teaspoon salt
½ cup chopped nuts—walnuts, pecans, or peanuts
⅓ cup butter or other shortening, melted*
1 cup firmly packed brown sugar
1 egg, slightly beaten
1 teaspoon vanilla
½ cup Baker's Semi-Sweet Chocolate Chips

• Sift flour once, measure, add baking powder, soda and salt, and sift again; add nuts. Mix melted shortening with sugar. Cool slightly. Add egg and vanilla. Add flour mixture, small amount at a time, mixing well after each addition. Spread in a greased 9x9x2-inch pan. Sprinkle chocolate chips over top. Bake in moderate oven (350° F.) 20 to 25 minutes. (Do not overbake.) Cool in pan. Then cut in 1½x2¼-inch bars. Makes 2 dozen bars.

* *When vegetable shortening is used, add 1 tablespoon hot water after the brown sugar.*

Chocolate Chip Oatmeal Cookies

⅔ cup sifted flour
½ teaspoon Calumet Baking Powder
1 cup quick-cooking rolled oats
¾ cup butter or other shortening
½ cup granulated sugar
¼ cup firmly packed brown sugar
1 egg
½ cup chopped salted peanuts
1 cup (6 ounces) Baker's Semi-Sweet Chocolate Chips

• Sift flour once, measure, add the baking powder, and sift again. Add rolled oats and mix well. Cream shortening until soft. Add sugars gradually and cream together until light and fluffy. Add egg and blend. Add dry ingredients gradually, mixing thoroughly. Then add peanuts and chocolate chips; mix well. Drop from teaspoon on ungreased baking sheet. Press flat with a fork. Bake in moderate oven (375° F.) 13 or 14 minutes. Allow cookies to stand on baking sheet about ½ minute; then remove and cool on rack. Makes about 3 dozen.

Chocolate Coconut Cups

1 cup (6 ounces) Baker's Semi-Sweet Chocolate Chips
1⅓ cups (about) Baker's Coconut
Vanilla ice cream
Peppermint ice cream

• Melt chocolate chips over hot (not boiling) water. Remove from hot water. Stir in coconut. Place paper cup-cake liners in muffin tins. Set aside about 6 tablespoons of the mixture. Press remainder around sides and over bottoms of paper liners. Then using 1 tablespoon of the chocolate-coconut mixture per cup, make a chocolate partition across the center of each, pressing firmly against sides and bottom. (Mixture is thick enough to hold shape.) Chill about 1 hour. Then remove paper cups and chill until ready to serve. Makes 6 cups.

Just before serving, fill one side of cups with vanilla ice cream and the other side with the peppermint. Also suggested are: butter pecan and maple, almond crunch and vanilla, peach and strawberry, and chocolate with orange sherbet.

Chocolate Chip Ice Cream

2 egg whites
¼ cup sugar
Dash of salt
1 cup heavy cream
2 egg yolks
½ teaspoon vanilla
½ cup Baker's Semi-Sweet Chocolate Chips, chopped

• Beat egg whites until foamy throughout. Add 2 tablespoons sugar gradually and continue beating until mixture will stand in moist peaks. Add remaining sugar and salt to cream and whip until thick; add egg yolks and beat only until blended. Add vanilla. Fold in egg whites. Add chocolate last, mixing lightly. Turn into tray of automatic refrigerator, setting control for coldest freezing temperature. Freeze until firm. Freezing time: 2 to 3 hours. Makes about 1 quart ice cream.

Chocolate Chip Peppermint Ice Cream

• Use recipe for Chocolate Chip Ice Cream (above), adding ½ to ¾ teaspoon peppermint extract instead of vanilla.

Chocolate Fleck Cake (3 egg whites)

2 1/4 cups sifted Swans Down Cake Flour
2 1/4 teaspoons Calumet Baking Powder
1/2 teaspoon salt
1/2 cup butter or other shortening
1 cup sugar
3 egg whites, unbeaten
3/4 cup milk
1 1/2 teaspoons vanilla
1 cup (6 ounces) Baker's Semi-Sweet Chocolate Chips

• Sift flour once, measure, add baking powder and salt, and sift together three times. Cream shortening, add sugar gradually, and cream together until light and fluffy. Add egg whites, one at a time, beating thoroughly after each. Add flour, alternately with milk, a small amount at a time, beating after each addition until smooth. Add vanilla. Grease 10x10x2-inch pan, line with waxed paper, and grease again. Pour about 1/3 of batter into pan. Sprinkle 1/3 of chocolate over top. Repeat twice, ending with chocolate. Bake in moderate oven (350° F.) 40 minutes, or until done. Spread Brown Velvet Frosting (below) on top of cake. Or serve unfrosted.

To make cup cakes, add chocolate to cake batter with vanilla. Bake in greased cup-cake pans in moderate oven (375° F.) 20 minutes, or until done. Makes 30 cup cakes. Top with Seven Minute Frosting (page 73) or whipped cream.

Chocolate Chip Frosting

2 baked 8-inch cake layers
2 cups (12 ounces) Baker's Semi-Sweet Chocolate Chips

• Place layers on baking sheet, having one layer top-side down. Cover tops of cakes with chips. Heat in moderate oven (350° F.) 6 minutes, or until chips are just softened. Remove from oven. Spread softened chips over bottom layer, letting chocolate run down on sides. Arrange top layer and spread as before. Then spread sides evenly. If frosting loses its gloss, before serving place cake in moderate oven (350° F.) 1 to 2 minutes to heat chocolate slightly.

To cover tops of cake only, use 1 cup (6 ounces) Baker's Semi-Sweet Chocolate Chips.

Note: If desired, the chocolate chips may be melted over hot water, then spread on top and sides of cake.

Chocolate Chip Seven Minute Frosting

• Use recipe for Seven Minute Frosting or Fluffy Seven Minute Frosting (page 73). Before spreading, fold in 1 package Baker's Semi-Sweet Chocolate Chips.

Note: Frosting should be sufficiently cool to prevent melting and streaking of chocolate before chips are added.

Brown Velvet Frosting

1 package Baker's Semi-Sweet Chocolate Chips
¼ cup butter or margarine
Dash of salt
1 cup evaporated milk
2¼ cups sifted confectioners' sugar
½ teaspoon vanilla

• Melt chocolate and butter in saucepan. Remove from heat. Add salt, milk, and 1 cup of the sugar; mix well. Bring to a boil over medium heat, stirring constantly. Then cook and stir 8 minutes. Remove from heat and add vanilla; blend. Cool to room temperature. Add the remaining 1¼ cups sugar in small amounts, blending well. Makes 2¼ cups frosting, or enough to cover tops and sides of two 8-inch layers.

Chocolate Chip Orange Drops

1 cup sifted flour
¼ teaspoon salt
½ cup butter or other shortening
3 ounces (1 package) cream cheese
1 teaspoon grated orange rind
½ cup sugar
1 egg yolk
1 teaspoon vanilla
1 package Baker's Semi-Sweet Chocolate Chips

• Sift flour once, measure, add salt and sift again. Cream together shortening, cheese, and orange rind. Add sugar, egg yolk, and vanilla and beat until light; add flour and mix only until blended; then add chocolate chips and mix well. Drop from teaspoon on lightly greased baking sheet. Flatten with back of spoon. Bake in moderate oven (350° F.) 15 minutes. Makes 3 dozen drops.

Chocolate Nut Squares

1 cup sifted flour
1 teaspoon Calumet Baking Powder
½ teaspoon salt
1 cup sugar
2 eggs, well beaten
1 teaspoon vanilla
1 tablespoon melted butter or other shortening
1 tablespoon hot water
1 cup broken nut meats
1 cup (6 ounces) Baker's Semi-Sweet Chocolate Chips

• Sift flour once, measure, add baking powder and salt, and sift again. Add sugar gradually to egg, beating well. Add vanilla, butter, and water; then add nuts and chocolate chips. Add flour gradually, mixing well. Turn into a well-greased 13x9x2-inch pan. Bake in a slow oven (325° F.) 30 to 35 minutes. Cool. Cut into 1½-inch squares. Makes 40 squares.

Chocolate Date Bars

• Use recipe for Chocolate Nut Squares (above). Add ½ cup dates, seeded and finely cut; decrease nut meats to ½ cup.

Uncooked Fudge

½ cup sweetened condensed milk
1 cup (6 ounces) Baker's Semi-Sweet Chocolate Chips, melted
½ teaspoon vanilla

• Add milk gradually to melted chips over hot water; stir to blend. Remove from heat; add vanilla. Turn into greased 8x4-inch pan. Chill. Cut in squares. Makes 21 pieces.

Chocolate Fluff Topping

2 egg whites
⅛ teaspoon salt
⅓ cup corn syrup
½ cup Baker's Semi-Sweet Chocolate Chips, melted
1 teaspoon vanilla

• Beat egg whites with salt until stiff enough to hold up in peaks, but not dry. Add syrup gradually; continue beating until very thick. Fold in chocolate and vanilla. Makes 2 cups.

Chocolate Fudge Sauce

1 cup (6 ounces) Baker's Semi-Sweet Chocolate Chips
3 tablespoons water
4 tablespoons light cream

• Melt chocolate in 3 tablespoons water over low heat. Stir to blend. Remove from heat. Blend in cream. Serve hot or cold on ice cream, cake, or pudding. Makes 1 cup sauce. Sauce may be kept, covered, in refrigerator and reheated over hot water as needed. Will keep for several days.

Chocolate Clusters

½ cup Baker's Semi-Sweet Chocolate Chips
⅔ cup raisins or roasted peanuts, skinned

• Heat chocolate over hot water until partly melted; then remove from hot water and stir rapidly until entirely melted. Add raisins or nuts and mix well. Drop from teaspoon on waxed paper. Chill until firm. Makes 12 clusters.

Coconut Clusters. Substitute ½ cup Baker's Coconut instead of the raisins or peanuts in this recipe.

Chocolate Marshmallow Clusters. Substitute 6 marshmallows, cut in eighths, for raisins or peanuts in this recipe.

Chocolate Toasties Clusters. Substitute ⅔ cup of Post Toasties for raisins or peanuts in this recipe. Makes 9.

Chocolate Chip Peanut Butter Fudge

2 cups sugar
¾ cup milk
1 tablespoon butter
1 teaspoon vanilla
3 tablespoons peanut butter
½ cup Baker's Semi-Sweet Chocolate Chips

• Combine sugar and milk; bring to a boil, stirring constantly. Continue boiling, without stirring, until a small amount of mixture forms a soft ball in cold water (234° F.). Add butter and vanilla. Cool to lukewarm (110° F.). Then add peanut butter. Beat until mixture begins to thicken and loses its gloss. At once stir in chocolate chips; turn into greased pan, 8x4 inches. Cool; cut. Makes 18 pieces.

Recipes Made with Baker's German's Sweet Chocolate

Baker's German's Sweet Chocolate is a double-feature chocolate, delicious both as a confection and for making specialty chocolate dishes. You'll find recipes for some of these very special dishes in this section.

The German's Chocolate Cake is an example. Wherever it goes, people want the recipe. Cakemakers send it proudly to friends. Already the recipe is prized up and down this country and in Canada, too.

Angel Pie, page 96, is another wonderful Baker's German's dessert. Notice the different fillings you can make.

Once you know the smooth rich flavor of German's Chocolate you'll always want it on hand. It is a favorite eating chocolate, too, and makes a delightful drink.

German's Chocolate Cake

1 package Baker's German's Sweet Chocolate
½ cup boiling water
1 cup butter or other shortening
2 cups sugar
4 egg yolks, unbeaten
1 teaspoon vanilla
½ teaspoon salt
1 teaspoon soda
2½ cups sifted Swans Down Cake Flour
1 cup buttermilk
4 egg whites

• Melt chocolate in the boiling water. Cool. Cream butter and sugar until light and fluffy. Add egg yolks, one at a time, beating after each. Add chocolate and vanilla.

Sift together salt, soda, and flour. Add alternately with buttermilk to chocolate mixture, beating well after each addition. Then beat until batter is smooth.

Beat egg whites until very stiff peaks will form. Fold into batter. Pour into three 8- or 9-inch layer pans, lined on bottoms with paper. Bake in moderate oven (350° F.) 30 to 40 minutes. Or bake in two square 9x9x2-inch pans 40 to 45 minutes. Cool. Frost tops with Coconut-Pecan Frosting (below).

Coconut-Pecan Frosting

- 1 cup evaporated milk
- 1 cup sugar
- 3 egg yolks
- ¼ pound margarine
- 1 teaspoon vanilla
- 1⅓ cups Baker's Coconut
- 1 cup chopped pecans

• Combine evaporated milk, sugar, and egg yolks in a saucepan. Blend well and then add the margarine.

Cook over medium heat, stirring constantly, until mixture thickens—takes about 12 minutes. Remove from heat. Add vanilla and stir to blend. Add coconut and pecans.

Beat until the mixture is cool and thick enough to spread. Makes about 2⅔ cups, or enough frosting to cover the tops of three 8- or 9-inch round layers or two 9-inch squares.

Neighbor tells neighbor of this wonderful German's Chocolate Cake. So moist, delicate, delicious . . . the recipe is sweeping the country.

Chocolate Angel Pie

2 egg whites
1/8 teaspoon salt
1/8 teaspoon cream of tartar
1/2 cup sugar
1/2 cup finely chopped walnut or pecan meats
1/2 teaspoon vanilla

1 package (1/4 pound) Baker's German's Sweet Chocolate
3 tablespoons water
1 teaspoon vanilla
1 cup whipping cream

• Beat egg whites until foamy, add salt and cream of tartar. Add sugar, 2 tablespoons at a time, beating after each addition until blended. Continue beating until very stiff peaks will form. Fold in nuts and 1/2 teaspoon vanilla. Spoon into a lightly greased 8-inch pie pan and make a nest-like shell, building up the rim about 1/2 inch above edge of pan. Bake in a slow oven (300° F.) 50 to 55 minutes. Cool.

Combine chocolate and water in saucepan. Place over low heat and stir until chocolate melts. Cool until thickened. Add 1 teaspoon vanilla. Whip cream and fold in chocolate mixture. Spoon into meringue shell. Chill 2 hours.

Chocolate Whipped Cream Dessert

• Prepare chocolate mixture as for Chocolate Angel Pie (above). Pile lightly in sherbet glasses, lined with lady fingers or strips of sponge cake. Serves 4 to 5.

Mocha Angel Pie

• Use recipe for Chocolate Angel Pie (above). Add 1 teaspoon Instant Maxwell House Coffee to the melted chocolate.

Spicy Angel Pie

• Use recipe for Chocolate Angel Pie (above). Add 1/2 teaspoon cinnamon to the melted chocolate.

Piquant Angel Pie

• Use recipe for Chocolate Angel Pie (above). Add 1/2 teaspoon angostura bitters with the vanilla.

German's Chocolate Dew Drops

½ package (9 squares) Baker's German's Sweet Chocolate
1½ cups ground walnuts
¾ cup sugar
2 eggs
⅓ cup confectioners' sugar

• Melt chocolate over hot water and stir until smooth. Combine ground walnuts, sugar, 1 whole egg, and 1 egg yolk. Mix in melted chocolate. Drop by teaspoonfuls onto greased baking sheets. Flatten each cooky with a fork.

Beat the remaining egg white until soft peaks will form. Add sugar gradually, beating after each addition until sugar is well blended. Then continue beating until stiff peaks will form. Top each cooky with a dab of meringue. Bake in moderate oven (350° F.) for 20 minutes. Makes 2 to 2½ dozen.

Chocolate Marshmallow Top Hats

1 package (¼ pound) Baker's German's Sweet Chocolate
16 marshmallows
½ cup finely chopped walnuts or pecans

• Melt chocolate over hot water and stir rapidly until smooth. Cool slightly. Dip top of each marshmallow in chocolate and then in chopped nuts. Chill. Makes 16.

German's Sweet Chocolate Nut Squares

1 package (¼ pound) Baker's German's Sweet Chocolate
⅔ cup chopped walnuts

• Melt chocolate over hot (not boiling) water. Remove from hot water, add nuts, and mix well. Spread about ¼ inch thick on a cooky sheet. Chill. Cut into squares. Makes 24.

Chocolate Curl Sundae

• Use 1 package (¼ pound) Baker's German's Sweet Chocolate and with a small sharp knife or vegetable peeler shave thin chocolate curls with long slanted strokes. Serve on vanilla, peppermint, coffee, chocolate, or butter pecan ice cream. Good, too, as garnish for whipped cream desserts, frosted cakes, cream or chiffon pies, and cream puddings.

Sweet Chocolate Drink

½ package (9 squares) Baker's German's Sweet Chocolate
2 cups milk

• Add chocolate to milk and heat in double boiler. When chocolate is melted, beat with rotary egg beater until light and frothy. Serve immediately. If desired, top each serving with a marshmallow or spoonful of whipped cream. Makes 2 cups.

Note: One cup milk and 1 cup water may be used.

Quick Hot Fudge Sauce

1 package (¼ pound) Baker's German's Sweet Chocolate
3 marshmallows
¼ cup milk
Dash of salt

• Combine all ingredients in top of a double boiler. Cook and stir over hot water until chocolate and marshmallows melt and mixture is well blended. Serve over ice cream, cake squares, or puddings. Makes about ½ cup, or 3 servings.

Note: Sauce may be stored in covered glass jar in refrigerator and reheated just before serving.

Frozen Sundae

1 quart vanilla ice cream, softened
1 package (¼ pound) Baker's German's Sweet Chocolate
½ cup butter
2 tablespoons sifted confectioners' sugar
3 egg yolks
1 teaspoon vanilla
Dash of salt
3 egg whites
½ cup chopped nuts
½ cup crushed vanilla wafers (about 18)

• Place softened ice cream in two refrigerator trays. Freeze until hard. Meanwhile, melt chocolate and butter in saucepan over low heat. Add to sugar in mixing bowl. Add egg yolks, one at a time, beating well after each. Add vanilla and salt and beat well. Then beat egg whites until stiff peaks will form. Fold into chocolate mixture.

Sprinkle nuts over firm ice cream. Spread with chocolate mixture. Top with wafer crumbs. Freeze overnight. Serves 12.

Chocolate Icebox Cake

1 teaspoon gelatin
2 tablespoons sugar
Dash of salt
⅓ cup water
1 or 2 packages (¼ or ½ pound) Baker's German's Sweet Chocolate
2 egg yolks, slightly beaten
1 teaspoon vanilla
2 egg whites, stiffly beaten
½ cup whipping cream
½ cup finely cut walnuts
1½ dozen (36 split) ladyfingers

• Combine gelatin, sugar, and salt in top of double boiler. Add water and chocolate. Heat and stir over boiling water until chocolate is melted. Remove from boiling water and add beaten egg yolks, a little at a time, beating until well blended. Cook over boiling water for 2 minutes, stirring constantly. Add the vanilla; cool. Fold into egg whites. Chill. Whip cream and fold into the chilled chocolate mixture. Fold in nuts.
• Line bottom and sides of 1-quart mold with waxed paper. Arrange ladyfingers on bottom and sides of mold. Pour in half of chocolate mixture. Cover with ladyfingers. Then add rest of chocolate mixture and top with ladyfingers. Chill for 8 to 12 hours in refrigerator. Unmold. Makes 8 servings.

Note: For added flavor, walnuts may be lightly toasted in a little butter. Or, if desired nuts may be omitted.

Sally's Chocolate Sponge

1 package (¼ pound) Baker's German's Sweet Chocolate
3 tablespoons butter
⅓ cup sugar
Dash of salt
2 egg whites, stiffly beaten

• Melt chocolate in top of double boiler. Add butter and blend. Add sugar and salt and mix well. Cool slightly while beating egg whites. Stir chocolate mixture into egg whites, gently but thoroughly. Turn into custard cups. Place in pan of hot water and bake in moderate oven (375° F.) about 50 minutes. Serve hot with cream. Serves 4.

Recipes Made with Baker's Dot Chocolate

Perhaps you're hungry for some homemade candy or are looking for chocolate goodies that are easy to make. Then you have turned to the right section. Baker's Dot Chocolate has the answer.

Most of the delicious candies given here are simple as can be, yet they look and taste wonderfully expert.

Dot Chocolate, the chocolate made especially for candy making, solves your problem. It's the type of chocolate used by candy manufacturers—an extra-rich bittersweet chocolate that blends equally well with nuts, fruits, or fondant centers.

Many of the recipes given are "quickies" requiring an easy "pour-on" job. With others all you do is combine melted Dot Chocolate with a few other ingredients. You won't believe anything so good can be so simple until you try Brazil Nut or Raisin Nut Bars, Chocolate Coconut Glossies, or Chocolate Coconut Marshmallows.

Here, too, are recipes for candy specialties, the kind you can become famous for: Chocolate Peanut Brittle, Grand Operas, and Dot Molasses Taffy.

Next time you make up a gift box of candies, remember to use Dot Chocolate, the home candy maker's friend! It comes in 8-ounce cakes, deeply grooved in squares of 1-ounce each. These squares may be broken off easily as needed in recipes, or the whole cake melted.

Chocolate Coconut Marshmallows

8 squares Baker's Dot Chocolate
28 marshmallows (7 ounces), cut in halves
3 cups Baker's Premium Shred Coconut, toasted, or 1½ cups chopped nut meats

• Heat chocolate over boiling water until partly melted; then remove from boiling water and stir rapidly until entirely melted. Dip marshmallows in chocolate, one at a time, roll in coconut or nuts, and place on waxed paper. Cool until firm. Makes 4½ dozen chocolate marshmallows.

Grand Operas

2 cups sugar
¾ cup light cream
½ cup milk
1 tablespoon light corn syrup
⅛ teaspoon salt
1 teaspoon vanilla
¾ cup broken pecan meats
6 squares Baker's Dot Chocolate

• Combine sugar, cream, milk, corn syrup, and salt, and heat until sugar is dissolved and mixture boils, stirring constantly. Continue cooking, stirring frequently, until a small amount of syrup forms a soft ball in cold water (236° F.). Cool to lukewarm (110° F.) and add vanilla. Beat until mixture begins to thicken; then add nuts and continue beating only until mixture loses its gloss. Turn at once into greased pan, 8x8 inches. Let stand until thoroughly cold.

Heat chocolate over hot water until partly melted; then remove from hot water and stir rapidly until entirely melted. Pour over candy. Cool until firm. Cut in squares. Makes 64.

Chocolate Coconut Glossies

8 squares Baker's Dot Chocolate
⅔ cup sweetened condensed milk
1⅓ cups Baker's Coconut
1 teaspoon vanilla

• Heat chocolate over hot water until partly melted; then remove from hot water and stir rapidly until entirely melted. Add milk and blend; then add coconut and vanilla. Drop from teaspoon on waxed paper. Cool until firm. Makes 3 dozen.

Chocolate Ting-a-lings

8 squares Baker's Dot Chocolate
2 cups Post Toasties

• Heat chocolate over hot water until partly melted; then remove from hot water and stir rapidly until entirely melted. Add Toasties and mix lightly until the Toasties are completely coated with chocolate. Drop from teaspoon on waxed paper. Cool until firm. Makes 2½ dozen.

How to Make Dot Chocolate Bars

• Line bottom of loaf pan, 8x4 inches, with waxed paper, letting paper extend in 2-inch tabs at each end. Use nuts, fruit, or other ingredients as suggested in recipes below. Arrange or sprinkle these evenly over bottom of the pan.

Heat required amount of Dot Chocolate over boiling water until partly melted; then remove from boiling water and stir rapidly until entirely melted. Pour chocolate evenly over the ingredients in pan. If necessary, tap pan several times to settle chocolate. Let stand in cool place to harden. Lift entire chocolate block out of pan using the paper tabs. Cut in bars, 1x2 inches. Makes 16 bars. The illustrations below and on page 105 show how to make and cut bars.

Cashew Bars

¾ cup halved salted cashew meats
6 squares Baker's Dot Chocolate

• Place nuts in lined pan and cover with melted chocolate as directed (above). Additional whole cashew meats may be arranged on top, if desired. Cool and cut.

Peanut Bars

• Use recipe for Cashew Bars (above), substituting ¾ cup roasted peanuts, skinned, for cashew meats. Salted or unsalted peanuts may be used.

Toasted Almond Bars

• Use recipe for Cashew Bars (above), substituting ¾ cup blanched, toasted almonds for cashew meats. If unblanched almonds are used, they should be washed thoroughly, dried, and toasted.

Raisin Nut Bars

⅔ cup seedless raisins
⅔ cup broken walnut meats
8 squares Baker's Dot Chocolate

• Wash raisins in hot water and dry thoroughly. Place in lined pan and sprinkle with nuts. Cover with melted chocolate as directed (above). Cool and cut.

Fig Pecan Bars

⅔ cup finely cut dried figs
⅔ cup broken pecan meats
8 squares Baker's Dot Chocolate

• Mix figs and nuts until blended. Place in lined pan and cover with melted chocolate as directed (above). Cool and cut.

Chocolate Coconut Patties

8 squares Baker's Dot Chocolate
1¾ cups Baker's Premium Shred Coconut

• Heat chocolate over boiling water until partly melted; then remove from boiling water and stir rapidly until entirely melted. Add coconut and stir until blended. Drop from teaspoon on waxed paper. Cool until firm. Makes 2 dozen patties.

It's easy as this to make all kinds of Dot Chocolate Bars. Notice the handy way to line the pan! These will be Rocky Roads, page 104.

Rocky Road Bars

10 marshmallows, cut in quarters
½ cup broken walnut meats
8 squares Baker's Dot Chocolate

• Arrange marshmallows in pan and fill spaces between marshmallows with nuts. Cover with melted chocolate as directed (page 102). Cool and cut.

Toasties Marshmallow Bars

• Use recipe for Rocky Road Bars (above), substituting 1 cup Post's Toasties for walnut meats.

Puffed Rice Bars

1 cup puffed rice
8 squares Baker's Dot Chocolate

• Place puffed rice in pan and cover with melted chocolate as directed (page 102). Cool and cut.

Popcorn Bars

2 cups popcorn
8 squares Baker's Dot Chocolate

• Place popcorn in lined pan and cover with melted chocolate as directed (page 102). Cool and cut.

Stuffed Date Bars

16 dates, stuffed with peanut butter or nut meats
8 squares Baker's Dot Chocolate

• Arrange dates in rows in lined pan, having stuffed-side up. Cover with melted chocolate as directed (page 102). Cool; cut.

Animal Cracker Place Cards

8 squares Baker's Dot Chocolate
14 animal crackers

• Melt chocolate as directed (page 102). Pour into prepared pan. When partly firm, stand animal crackers in chocolate as shown (below). Cool and cut. Use as favors or place cards at children's party.

Tutti-frutti Bars

⅓ cup finely cut candied pineapple
⅓ cup finely cut candied cherries
⅓ cup finely cut citron
⅓ cup blanched almonds, cut and toasted
8 squares Baker's Dot Chocolate

• Mix fruit and nuts until blended. Place in lined pan and cover with melted chocolate as directed (page 102). Cool to harden. Cut in bars or squares.

Brazil Nut Bars

16 Brazil nut meats
8 squares Baker's Dot Chocolate

• Melt chocolate as directed (page 102). Pour into prepared pan. When partly firm, arrange nuts in rows. Cool and cut.

Like professional chocolate bars but twice as exciting are Animal Cracker Place Cards, Brazil Nut Bars, and Rocky Roads, all finished.

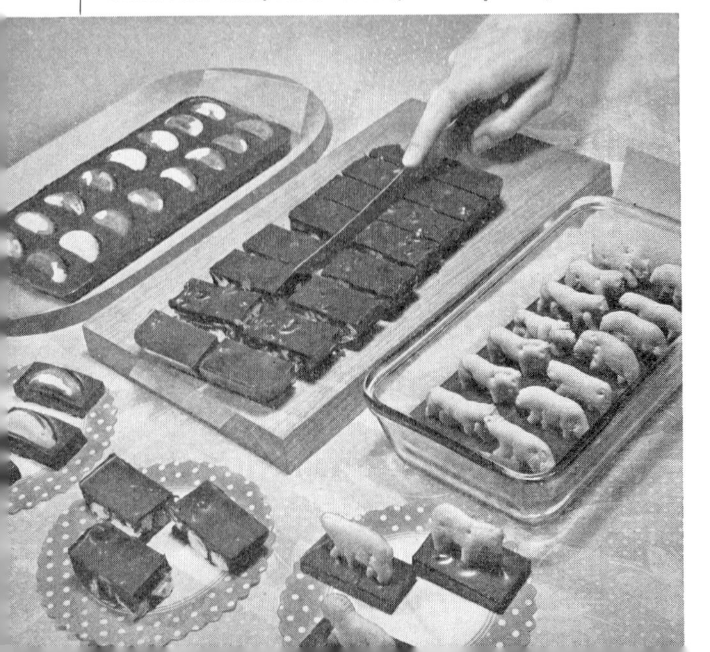

Chocolate Peanut Brittle

1½ cups sugar
⅔ cup water
½ cup light corn syrup
2 tablespoons butter
½ pound shelled peanuts
1 teaspoon soda
1 tablespoon cold water
1 teaspoon vanilla
8 squares Baker's Dot Chocolate

• Combine sugar, water, and corn syrup. Place over low flame and stir constantly until sugar is dissolved. Cook until a small amount of syrup becomes brittle in cold water (275° F.). Add butter and peanuts and stir until peanuts are slightly browned (296° F.). Dissolve soda in cold water, add vanilla, and stir slowly into candy. Pour out on warm, buttered baking sheet, 15x10 inches, spreading with spatula to cover pan and make even, if necessary. Cool.

Heat chocolate over boiling water until partly melted; then remove from boiling water and stir rapidly until entirely melted. Pour over candy. Cool until firm, then break into small pieces. Makes 1¾ pounds brittle.

Dot Molasses Taffy

4 squares Baker's Dot Chocolate
1 cup light brown sugar, firmly packed
⅓ cup corn syrup
⅔ cup water
1 cup light molasses
¼ teaspoon salt
2 tablespoons butter

• Combine chocolate, sugar, corn syrup, water, molasses, salt, and butter in saucepan. Place over low flame and stir constantly until mixture boils. Continue boiling, stirring frequently to prevent scorching, until a small amount of syrup forms a hard ball in cold water (262° F.). Pour on greased platter or marble slab. As candy cools on edges, fold edges toward center with spatula; continue folding until candy is cool enough to handle. Butter hands lightly and pull candy until cold. Stretch out in long rope and cut with scissors. Makes 5 dozen 1-inch pieces.

Timesaving Dishes made with Baker's Instant

If Baker's Instant has found its way to your house, you already know it makes wonderful chocolate drinks—hot or cold. And you'll have had a chance to try the quick-easy recipes on the package for frosting, fudge, and sauce.

Now, in addition, you'll want to try other popular ways to use this versatile cocoa mix. Here are Quick-Cook Fudge, a new toast idea, sauce, ice creams, rich dessert roll, and special chocolate drinks. You can add them to your list of handy-dandy recipes, because every one is easy to make and has delicious chocolate flavor.

Quick-Cook Fudge

½ cup Baker's Instant
1 cup sugar
3 tablespoons butter
¼ cup milk

• Have ready a greased plate or 8-inch pie pan. Combine ingredients in small saucepan. Cook and stir over medium heat until sugar is *completely dissolved*—about 5 minutes. Bring to a full rolling boil and cook for 1 minute without stirring. Remove from heat. Beat with spoon until the mixture begins to thicken—about 2 to 3 minutes. *At once* spread on the greased plate. Let stand 5 minutes; cut in 24 pieces. Cool.

Chocolate Cinnamon Toast

¼ cup Baker's Instant
⅓ cup sugar
1 teaspoon cinnamon
Buttered hot toast

• Combine Baker's Instant, sugar, and cinnamon; mix well. Sprinkle on hot buttered toast. Serve at once. Store leftover mixture in covered jar. Makes enough for 30 slices toast.

Note: For quantity service, mix the dry ingredients with 5 tablespoons butter, melted. Spread at once on unbuttered hot toast. (Mixture becomes thick on standing.)

Fudge Sauce

½ cup Baker's Instant
3 tablespoons butter
⅔ cup top milk or light cream
½ cup sifted confectioners' sugar

• Combine Baker's Instant, butter, and milk in saucepan. Place over low heat until ingredients are blended, stirring constantly. Add sugar and mix well. Bring to a boil and cook, stirring constantly, 5 minutes, or until thickened. Serve hot on ice cream, cake, or pudding.

To store, keep in the refrigerator and then heat slightly over hot water before serving. Makes 1 cup.

Chocolate Ripple Ice Cream

1 quart vanilla ice cream
⅓ cup cold Fudge Sauce (above)

• Turn half of softened ice cream into the freezing tray of automatic refrigerator. Pour half of the fudge sauce over ice cream. Cover with remaining ice cream; then swirl remaining sauce over top. With knife, cut through ice cream in zigzag course. Set control for coldest freezing temperature. Freeze 2 to 3 hours, or until firm. Makes 1 quart.

Butter pecan or other flavors of ice cream may be used.

Chocolate Peppermint Punch

1 cup Baker's Instant
2 quarts cold milk
1 quart peppermint ice cream

• Add Baker's Instant to cold milk in a punch bowl. Stir to blend. Chill. Just before serving, add ice cream by tablespoonfuls, allowing ice cream to float. Serves 8 to 12.

Note: For 4 to 6 servings, halve all ingredients.

Little "Potatoes"

• Use recipe for Chocolate Fondant (page 65). Mold mixture into miniature potato shapes, about 1 inch long. Roll candies in Baker's Instant, coating thoroughly on all sides.

For a spicy variation, add a dash of cinnamon to each tablespoon of Baker's Instant used.

Cocoa-Nog

¼ cup Baker's Instant
1 egg yolk, unbeaten
Dash of salt
2 cups chilled milk
1 egg white, stiffly beaten

• Combine Baker's Instant, egg yolk, and salt and beat with egg beater until blended. Then add milk gradually, stirring constantly. Fold into beaten egg white. Serve at once in tall glasses. Makes 3 or 4 servings.

Instant Hot Cocoa

• Measure into cup 2 to 3 heaping teaspoons Baker's Instant. Add hot milk to fill cup. Blend. Serves 1.

For a special treat, top with whipped cream or marshmallow.

You'll love Baker's Instant for jiffy quick cocoa or frosting . . . for fudge and sauce, too. You'll find grand recipes on these pages.

Chocolate Malted

1½ tablespoons Baker's Instant
1½ tablespoons malted milk powder
1 cup chilled milk

• Combine Baker's Instant and malted milk powder in tall glass. Add milk gradually, stirring constantly. Blend well or mix in shaker. Makes 1 serving.

For a richer drink, add a scoop of vanilla ice cream.

Cocoa Whipped Cream

½ cup heavy cream
2 tablespoons Baker's Instant
Dash of salt

• Chill cream, small bowl, and egg beater. Pour chilled cream into bowl; add Baker's Instant and salt. Chill 1 hour. Beat rapidly until cream begins to thicken. Then beat slowly until cream holds its shape. (Do not overbeat.)

Use as topping for cake or other desserts. Or use as filling for tea puffs or éclairs. Makes ¾ cup.

Double Chocolate Roll

• Double recipe for Cocoa Whipped Cream (above). Spread 18 round chocolate wafers (2¾ inches in diameter) with Cocoa Whipped Cream, using 1 heaping tablespoon on each wafer. Stand wafers on edge on platter and press together to form roll. Spread roll with remaining cream mixture. Chill 3 to 4 hours. Cut diagonally to serve. Makes 4 to 6 servings.

Chocolate Mousse

⅓ cup Baker's Instant
⅛ teaspoon salt
1 cup heavy cream
½ teaspoon vanilla
1 egg white, stiffly beaten

• Combine Baker's Instant, salt, cream, and vanilla. Chill 15 to 20 minutes. Then beat until mixture holds its shape. Fold in stiffly beaten egg white. Fill paper soufflé cups or molds with mixture. Place in freezing unit of automatic refrigerator, set control for coldest freezing temperature, and freeze 2 to 3 hours. Makes 5 servings.

Index of Recipes

Index